10 Other

REAL ESTATE INVESTMENTS YOU COULD DO

SECTION 121   BILLBOARDS
RAW LAND   STORAGE UNITS
WHOLESALING   NOTES
MOBILE HOMES   FLIPPING
PRIVATE   HARD MONEY
LENDING   LENDING

MICHAEL LANTRIP
Attorney | Accountant | Investor

THE AUTHOR

Michael Lantrip, Attorney at Law, is licensed to practice law in Texas, North Carolina, Virginia, and the District of Columbia.

He has a B.B.A. in Finance from the University of Houston School of Business, and he has a Juris Doctor (J.D.) in Law from the University of Texas School of Law.

He is admitted to practice in all Courts in Texas, North Carolina, Virginia, and the District of Columbia, as well as the U.S. Tax Court, the U.S. Federal District Court, and the D.C. Court of Appeals.

He is a member of The National Society of Accountants.

He practices in the fields of Tax Law, Real Estate Law, Corporate and Business Law, and Wills, Trusts and Estates.

Formerly a Tax Examiner for the IRS, and a Tax Accountant for a Big 8 Accounting Firm, he has also been a Newspaper Reporter, Radio Announcer, Radio News Director, Television Reporter and Anchorman, Television Executive News Producer, and Military Intelligence Analyst.

As an elected County Attorney, responsible for Criminal Misdemeanor Prosecution, he handled over 2,000 cases.

In addition to 40 years of practicing law, he built one of the first computerized Abstract Plants, and operated his own Title Insurance Company, becoming an Approved Title Attorney for seven national Title Insurance Underwriters. He has handled over 2,000 real estate closings.

Prior to his law career, he was a Radio Announcer at WQTE in Detroit during the "Motown" era, and he was a DJ at KIKK in Houston when it was named "Country Music Station of the Year" by Billboard Magazine.

He collects and refurbishes Vintage Audio Equipment.

He has written and produced over 1,000 half-hour Television Newscasts.

He has written over 700 stories as a daily Newspaper Reporter.

He has logged over 8,000 hours on the radio.

He is a Lifetime Member of Mensa.

As a Real Estate Investor, his activities have ranged from travel trailers to office buildings, and from on-campus condos to rural land.

He has been named a Top Writer by Quora.com where his Answers have more than 2,630,000 views.

He has written and published 9 books.

1.) "How To Do A Section 1031 Like Kind Exchange,"

2.) "OMNIBUS EDITION How To Do A Section 1031 Like Kind Exchange"

3.) "50 Real Estate Investing Calculations,"

4.) "Tax Cuts And Jobs Act For Real Estate Investors,"

5.) "Your Best Business Entity For Real Estate Investing,"

6.) "10 Real Estate Investments You Could Do," and

7.) "Real Estate Investing Vocabulary of Terms."

8.) "Section 121 Real Estate Investing System"

9.) "Do This, Not That!"

All are available in print and digital on Amazon.

His Amazon Author Page is:

Amazon.com/author/michaellantrip.

His Personal website is MichaelLantrip.com.

His Quora page is www.quora.com/profile/Michael-Lantrip-1.

INTRODUCTION

The term "Real Estate Investing" doesn't only refer to buying a Single Family Residence (SFR) and turning it into a rent house, even though that is the most common scenario.

In fact, many Real Estate Investors make a comfortable income from real estate without ever dealing with a tenant or a toilet. They have found the ideal investment vehicle to fit their lifestyle.

And it might be different for each one.

Those Storage Units that you drove by yesterday are owned by a Real Estate Investor who is collecting monthly rent.

That Billboard where you read the advertisement about the local bank's new credit card is owned by a Real Estate Investor who is collecting monthly rent from the bank.

That house being rehabbed down the block has probably already provided income to a Wholesaler who assigned his contract to a House Flipper, who borrowed funds from a Hard Money Lender to buy and rehab, and then sold it to a Section 121 Investor, who financed it through a Private Money Lender, and when it was originally bought, the existing mortgage that was paid off might have been owned by a Note Investor.

Well, unlikely, but you get the idea.

All of these investors are part of the system.

The Real Estate Investing community is a diverse, dynamic collection of individuals, doing whatever fits the lifestyle of each one.

I've had clients engaged in almost all of these activities, some more than one, and I've done some of them myself and plan to do more. You need to know about them.

You can go with one of these Investments, or you can do more than one at a time. Most likely, you will progress from one to the other as your career moves forward.

But you must learn about them first.

And understanding how all of the others work will make you much more successful with the one you choose.

The sooner you get involved, the sooner you will realize that this is something that will change your life, and will show you a world you never imagined.

That's not an exaggeration.

I've seen it.

Even if you're already on the path that you planned for yourself, you need to take a look at the 10 Other Real Estate Investments.

Doctors and Engineers and Business Executives, along with other highly-compensated professionals are switching to Real Estate Investing every day.

Don't you think there might be something here for you to consider?

Now understand, this book is not intended as a blueprint for starting each of these businesses. It would be over two thousand pages.

With this book, I have tried to give you enough information about each aspect of Real Estate Investing to help you determine where you might fit, and figure out your direction. I've also corrected some misinformation that might lead you astray. And I have not included types that it would be impractical for you to consider, like warehouses, shopping centers, and office buildings.

With this book, you can get up in the morning, brew a pot of coffee, sit down at your kitchen table, and start laying out your plan of discovery and action.

Look at how each type of investment is done, picture yourself and your current lifestyle, and see if you can find a possible fit and direction.

This could be your "jumping off point" to the rest of your life.

Be careful, go slow, and Good Luck!

A short personal note here.

I don't do Email Marketing or social media. They are very time-consuming, and I prefer to spend my time writing.

So, I won't be bothering you or asking for your email.

But here's mine: Michael@MichaelLantrip.com.

I hope to hear from you if you have a question or comment.

This is all about you.

Are you ready?

Here are the subjects that I will cover.

CHAPTER 1 – HARD MONEY LENDING. Hard Money Lending (HML) involves making short-term loans, usually six months or less, to Real Estate Investors who are buying and rehabbing property, and who cannot qualify for, or cannot wait for, the loans available through regular lenders. For providing quick approval and funding, the HML lender can enjoy up to a 24% return, with a first lien position, if the project is successful, and up to a 45% return if the project fails. It is high return, low risk investing.

CHAPTER 2 – PRIVATE LENDING. The Private Money Lender will be operating in the space between the Hard Money Lender and the Bank. He will have no competition. The interest rate will be lower, usually 7-10%, and the term of the loan will be longer, usually one to five years. It is a more passive type of investing, but still low risk and good yield, with a first lien position just like a Bank.

CHAPTER 3 – NOTES. Note investing involves buying the Real Estate Lien Note, or the appropriate instrument where you are located, and receiving the payments due under the terms of the Note. The debt is secured by a first lien on the real property, so you can foreclose and take the property in case of default. You buy the Note for less than the Remaining Balance due on the Note and thereby increase your return to more than the stated interest rate on the Note.

CHAPTER 4 – WHOLESALING. "Wholesaling" is the inaccurate term applied to the signing of a Purchase Agreement with the owner of real property and then assigning the contract interest to a third part in return for a fee.

CHAPTER 5 – FLIPPING. Flipping is the practice of buying real estate, rehabbing it, and then either selling it for a profit, or putting permanent financing on it and holding it as rental property.

CHAPTER 6 – SECTION 121 INVESTING. Section 121 Investing is based on Section 121 of the Internal Revenue Code, which allows the Taxpayer to sell a personal residence lived in for two of the prior five years, and exempt all of the Capital Gains from taxation. The Taxpayer can use the house for rental property for three of those five years, and the Capital Gains accrued during these three years is also exempted from taxation.

CHAPTER 7 – MOBILE HOMES. Mobile Homes enjoy many advantages over regular residential real estate. They can be taxed either as real property or personal property. They can be bought and sold sometimes just by using a Title, like a vehicle. And because of the very low prices for used units, almost anyone can afford to become an investor.

CHAPTER 8 – BILLBOARDS. Billboards are exactly what you think they are. You see them along the roads and highways. Each Billboard must have a Permit, and the licensing process is governed by the federal and state governments, as well as the city or county where the Billboard is located. The value often depends on the traffic count of vehicles passing the location, and whether any new permits are being allowed. You can build new ones or buy existing ones. Depending on your area of the country, this could be your best investment.

CHAPTER 9 – STORAGE UNITS. The Storage Units that we discuss are not the huge complexes that you see along the highways. There are 40,000 facilities in the U.S. and about 90% are owned by medium and small investors. About 65% of the owners own a single facility, and only 25% own two or three. So there is room for the small investor. And this is the only real estate investment that does not have problems in an economic downturn, and it usually benefits from the disruption in business and personal lives.

CHAPTER 10 – RAW LAND. Land Investing is totally different from all other forms of Real Estate Investing. There is no building or structure involved so it is easier to evaluate, purchase, and manage. And it is the only one that you can divide up and make 10 (or more) properties from one. You can also lower your property taxes to almost nothing by obtaining a Timber or Agriculture classification. Land is also a good permanent store of wealth, and one of the best long-term investments you will find.

CHAPTER 11 – CHARGING ORDERS. This is an extra Chapter that will explain the benefit of using an LLC for your business entity for investing. The Charging Order protection is what makes it work. But it matters which State you reside in, and I have given you some information about how to deal with that problem as well.

CHAPTER 12 – CONCLUSION. A personal note.

COPYRIGHT PAGE

The Author has taken reasonable precautions in the preparation of this book and believes that the information presented in the book is accurate as of the date it was written. However, neither the Author nor the Publisher assumes any responsibility for any errors or omissions. The Author and the Publisher specifically disclaim any liability resulting from the use or application of the information contained in this book, and the information is not intended to serve as legal, tax, or other financial advice related to individual situations.

DISCLAIMER

Although I am a lawyer, I am not your lawyer. I would be honored if I were, but I am not.

Reading this book does not create an attorney-client relationship between us. This book should not be used as a substitute for the advice of a competent attorney admitted or authorized to practice law in your jurisdiction.

CONTENTS

CHAPTER 1

HARD MONEY LENDING

OVERVIEW

Hard Money Lending, known as HML, is my favorite of the Ten Other Real Estate Investments.

If the project goes as planned, you could enjoy a 20% Return On Investment (ROI), and if the project fails, you could make 40% (see "Foreclosure" below).

Money is the only thing that you have invested, and if you secured it correctly, you'll get all of that back.

Hard Money Lending is unique in the world of Real Estate Investing.

You don't own any property, and you won't do any of the work, but you will receive a very high return on your investment, with very low risk. This is due to the huge benefits available to the other Real Estate Investors that you'll be working with.

In simplified form, this is what you will be doing as a Hard Money Lender.

1

1.) A Real Estate Investor finds a property that he believes he can buy for $40,000 if he acts quickly, and that he can rehab for $20,000, and which will have an After Repair Value (ARV) of $100,000. But he doesn't have all of the $60,000 that he needs to buy and rehab the property. And he can't wait for, or can't qualify for, a bank loan. So he comes to you.

2.) You review his Purchase Agreement, inspect and photograph the property, and verbally agree to loan him $30,000 of the purchase price if he provides the other $10,000 of his own money as a Down Payment (just to make sure he is committed to the project; never loan money to people who are broke), and you also agree to loan him all of the $20,000 repair costs, for a total of $50,000, for six months at a rate of 10% (for the six months, not Annual Percentage Rate), plus two points, everything conditioned on him qualifying on your Loan Application and providing you with other required items.

3.) The Real Estate Investor, now called the Borrower, orders a Title Policy Commitment and a Survey, and provides you with current tax certificates. He also provides you a Broker's Price Opinion (BPO) on the ARV of the property, and what is called in the business a Statement of Work (SOW), which lists in detail the work that he plans to do on the property, in what order, and the cost of labor and materials.

4.) It turns out that title is clear, taxes are not delinquent, and the Borrower qualifies on your Loan Application. The Closing takes place. The property is deeded to the Borrower, and the Borrower signs a Real Estate Lien Note to you for $50,000 with specific terms, and a Deed of Trust creating a lien on the property securing your Note.

5.) At the Closing, the Seller receives his Net Sales Proceeds of $40,000 less his transaction costs. You provide $30,000 of the purchase price, and the Borrower provides the remaining $10,000. Your Closing Instructions to the Title Company tell them to write a check back to you for the remaining $20,000 of the funds that you provided for Closing, and to identify the funds as "Construction Draw Account."

6.) Then, outside Closing, you write a check to the Borrower for the first draw on the construction, between $5,000 and $10,000, depending on the SOW.

7.) As each phase of construction is completed, the Borrower calls you, you inspect and photograph the work, scan or photograph the receipts for material and the checks for the labor, and write the Borrower a draw check for the next phase of construction.

8.) When the project is complete, the Borrower will either sell the property for cash, or he will refinance the property and hold it as an investment.

9.) You will provide the Title Company with a Payoff Amount of $56,000, which is made up of $50,000 principal and $6,000 for interest and points. When you receive your check, you will sign a Release of Deed of Trust Lien.

You take your $56,000 and move on to the next deal.

If this deal went well, you might even fund the next deal of the same Borrower.

There will always be variations on the theme, but this is the theme.

Now, let's break this down and look at the normal elements of Real Estate Investing and see how each of the elements works for Hard Money Lending.

Those elements are:

1.) Income.

2.) Expenses.

3.) Cash Flow.

4.) Appreciation.

5.) Leverage.

6.) Tax Advantages.

INCOME

The income, as I described above, will be the interest and the points that you charge on the loan.

First, the points.

If you charge two points on a $50,000 loan, you will receive $1,000.

A point is one percentage point. Two points is 2%. Two Percent of $50,000 is $1,000.

Points are **not** based on the annual time frame, like interest rates are. Points are based on the loan amount.

Two points on a $50,000 loan for a period of one year is $1,000.

Two points on a $50,000 loan for only three months is also $1,000.

Point are a fee charged for making the loan, regardless of its duration.

For most loans, the points are collected from the Borrower, and paid to the Lender, at the Closing on the loan.

But for Hard Money Lending, you don't usually require this, and there are two reasons.

First, the Borrower probably doesn't have the $1,000 to pay you, that's why he's borrowing money from you.

Second, he is not buying a property that will begin to cash flow immediately, and he will not have money coming in. So even if he has $1,000, you want him to keep it so that he has a little cushion.

Now, the interest.

You want to make your loans for a six-month period because that will allow you to manage your business in the most efficient way.

You state your interest rate for the six-month period, so the Real Estate Investor will know exactly how much he is paying for money, and he can add it to his projected list of expenses, just like the counter tops and bathroom fixtures. If the loan is paid off early, it is still the same amount as for the full period.

If you make one $50,000 loan each month for the next six months, you will have $300,000 "on the street."

At the end of six months, you will have a loan being paid back each month and a new loan being made with the returned principal, so you will never have more than $300,000 out.

And you will be collecting $6,000 in interest and points each month.

That's $72,000 return per year on a $300,000 investment.

Your annual ROI is 24%.

Sometimes you will have a very good low-risk Borrower, and you will reduce his interest rate to 8% in order to keep him.

And sometimes you will have a first-time Borrower with no track record, but you believe in him, and you will require that he pay 12% until he proves himself.

But, on average, you should be able to earn 20-24% ROI.

EXPENSES

I am assuming that you already have the money to fund the loan, so I am not calculating cost of capital as one of your expenses. See "Leverage" below if you intend to use other people's money, or even borrow the funds that you intend to loan.

I am also not including the cost of organizing your business entity. See "Business Entity" below for that information.

So, you will have two other expenses: the expense of operating your business, and the expense of transaction on each loan.

First, the loan expenses.

The Borrower and the Seller will be splitting the expenses of transferring the property and closing the transaction. Your only costs will be to pay for the preparation of the Real Estate Lien Note and the Deed of Trust, because those are the only items in the transaction and in the Closing that involve your interest in the deal and for which you are responsible. You can require in your Loan Agreement with the Borrower that he pays for the preparation of these documents at Closing since they are part of his costs for obtaining a loan, but you should not allow either the Borrower or the Title Company to arrange for the preparation of these documents. This is where you and your Attorney work closely together and make sure that these documents contain all of the terms that you need to protect your interest in the deal. I cover that below in "The Loan."

The other expense, the expense of operating your business, will vary depending on how you set up and manage your business.

If this is your first business, you will need whatever tools that a new business usually requires.

I don't have the space to list all of those here, but there are some good resources on the internet for explaining how to set up a new business.

If you already have one or more businesses, then you can probably just use the tools and equipment that you already have. I don't know what you have, so I don't know what you need.

However, I would suggest that you have a good reliable vehicle. It should have off-road capability if you can afford that, because you will be visiting construction sites and, even if they are in the city, they might still be in rough shape during the rehab process.

I find that a Toyota 4Runner suits my needs very well, and it also provides a comfortable interior for meeting with the Borrower when visiting the job site, copying receipts, signing documents, and writing checks.

You should also have a small digital camera that will fit in your pocket. Make sure that the SD card will hold at least 1,000 images. You will use it to take photos of the property when you first look at it, and again after each phase of construction. You can just leave the images in the camera. Keep the digital camera in a safe place.

Other than equipment and tools, your expenses of operation will be whatever you decide to spend.

CASH FLOW

Your cash flow will be the same as your income. See above.

APPRECIATION

Since you will not be taking title to any real estate, appreciation does not really figure into the calculation.

The six-month duration of the loan will not be long enough for market value to increase, but the appreciation caused by rehabbing the property will increase the market value of the property, and therefore increase the amount of security that you have for your loan.

So, the appreciation that takes place is called "forced appreciation."

LEVERAGE

Leverage is a Real Estate Investing term for when you purchase a $100,000 property with $20,000 of your own money, and a loan of $80,000. The $80,000 is the leverage that you are using.

You own the entire $100,000 property and you will receive all of the increase in market value of the $100,000 property, even though you only invested $20,000 of your own money.

Leverage doesn't really apply in the Hard Money Lending business, even if you use borrowed money to fund your loans. We are probably dealing more with a concept called "float."

Float is the difference between what the funds are costing you, and the return that you are receiving from investing them.

The Hard Money Lending business model is more suited for someone who has funds to loan, but it can work for anyone who can get the funds.

TAX ADVANTAGES

Since Hard Money Lending is <u>not</u> the typical real estate investment, there are none of the usual tax advantages that are available to other Real Estate Investors.

BUSINESS ENTITY

You should never engage in business activities without first creating a business entity.

If you engage in business as an individual, you are subjecting yourself and your family, and all of your assets, for now and forever into the future, to the possibility of being sued and have a judgment entered against you, and then living at a subsistence level for the rest of your life.

Scared? You should be.

But the good news is that the law is on your side.

You just have to understand it, and know how to use it.

CHOICES

The business entities available to you for real estate investing, and for Hard Money Lending as a business, are:

1.) Limited Liability Company (LLC),

2.) Subchapter S Corporation (S Corp),

3.) Regular C Corporation (C Corp),

4.) Partnership (both General and Limited), and

5.) Sole Proprietorship (DBA).

You can study all of these in my book, "How To Choose Your Best Business Entity For Real Estate Investing: LLC, S Corp, C Corp, Partnership, or DBA?" It was published in early 2019 and will be updated for 2020, and it is available at www.Amazon.com/dp/B07MPQC295.

But, for now, I can tell you that the best Business Entity for Hard Money Lending is the LLC.

More accurately, the LLC in which you elect to be taxed as an S Corp.

LLC

The LLC is the best thing to happen to Real Estate Investors since the creation of the Subchapter S Corporation (S Corp) many years ago. The S Corp made it possible to have the liability protection of a C Corporation without the double taxation.

The LLC provides the same protection, and the same tax advantages.

And it adds the bonus of Charging Order protection.

You need to know about Charging Orders, so I have included a complete Chapter 11 on the subject. Be sure to read it. You might want to do that now.

The LLC is created by filing Articles of Organization with the State where you will be doing business. If you live in a State with weak Charging Order protection, you can set up your LLC in a State with strong Charging Order protection built into their laws, like Delaware, Nevada, Wyoming, or Texas, and then just qualify the LLC (called a "foreign entity") to do business wherever you are, by filing the required forms with your State agency.

Now, you still have to follow the laws of the State where you set up and are doing business, but your LLC will be dealt with under the laws of the State of formation, hopefully.

The LLC is owned by the Members.

The LLC is managed by either the Members, or by one or more persons designated by the Members to be the Manager. You will want to elect in the Articles of Organization when you file to create the LLC, to be a "Member Managed" LLC. That just means that you'll be managing everything.

The agreement between the various Members, and between the Members and the LLC, is a contract called the Operating Agreement.

Even if you are the only Member, you will still want an Operating Agreement. Without it, your LLC will be subject to the LLC laws of your State, and none of them are very good.

The Operating Agreement that I created recently for my Texas LLCs is 22 pages long, and much of the language involves choosing terms and conditions under which the LLC will operate that are different from those imposed by the Texas Business Organizations Code (BOC) for LLCs that do not declare their own operating provisions.

The Operating Agreement is one of the expenses of setting up your business that will be a one-time event, and could cost you about a thousand dollars. But it is critical that you get it right.

And don't go to just any Attorney. They all can "draft" an Operating Agreement for you with the software they have, which just assembles it and prints it out. And they believe they are doing the right thing. They just don't know what they don't know.

Go to an Attorney who practices primarily in the area of business, taxes, accounting, and Real Estate Investing. Tell him what you want and ask him if he can do a good job for you. If he is the right one, he will not be offended by your questions. He'll understand why you are asking.

And he'll create an Operating Agreement that is tailored to your specific situation, because he understands what you need. And the Operating Agreement will be written so that you can understand it, not the canned forms that come out of legal software programs that just assemble the various elements.

Like the Partnership and the S Corp, the LLC is a Pass-Through Entity (PTE).

That means that the business is not taxed on the income of the business. The income of the business "passes through" the business to the owner of the business, and the owner is taxed on the income.

So, although you are the owner of a Business Entity called an LLC, the income will be taxable to you personally instead of the Business Entity, along with your other income.

And you even get to select how you want the IRS to tax you.

You have two choices:

1.) As a Disregarded Entity, or

2.) As a Subchapter S Corporation (S Corp).

DISREGARDED ENTITY

After you create your LLC, you have the opportunity to file a form with the IRS, electing how you want to be taxed.

The form is Form 8832 Entity Classification Election.

You can see the form and read the Instructions at irs.gov/pub/irs-pdf/f8832.pdf.

Your options for classifying your entity for tax purposes are:

1.) a corporation,

2.) a partnership, or

3.) "an entity disregarded as separate from its owner."

This third choice is usually referred to as a Disregarded Entity.

If you do not file Form 8832, the default classification of your LLC will be a Disregarded Entity.

Here's what that means.

You will report the income and expenses of the business on Schedule C, and the taxable income will be transferred to your Form 1040 and taxed as ordinary income. It will also be classified as Self-Employment Income and will be taxed again at 15.3%.

You will probably, however, be able to exclude 20% of the income from taxation as Section 199A Qualified Business Income (QBI). This is a new law and the finer points are still being worked out.

I can recommend a book that I wrote last year, and updated this year, called "Tax Cuts and Jobs Act For Real Estate Investors: The New Rules." It is available from Amazon in digital and print at amazon.com/dp/B07D6T4P5J.

If you choose to be taxed as a Disregarded Entity, the LLC itself does not file a federal tax return.

Your State might have some different rules, and you can probably learn what they are by visiting the website of the taxing authority in your State.

If you would like to avoid a large portion of the 15.3% Self-Employment tax, read about the S Corp. next.

S CORP

If you file Form 8832 Entity Classification Election, you can choose to be taxed as a C Corporation, or as a Partnership.

Of course, you can also choose to be taxed as a Disregarded Entity, which is how you will be taxed if you don't file the form.

This is an example of IRS logic.

And there's more.

But first, let me tell you what a Subchapter S Corporation (S Corp) is.

It is not a corporation.

There is only one corporation, it is the C Corporation (C Corp).

The C Corp is the standard corporation, the kind that you see everywhere, like General Electric, General Motors, etc. Those are corporations, C Corporations.

The C Corp pays income taxes at the corporate level. Corporate taxes have just been lowered to 21% in the new Tax Cuts And Jobs Act (TCJA).

After the C Corp pays its taxes, the after-tax income is usually distributed to the stockholders in the form of a Dividend. The amount of the Dividend is then taxed again to the individual who received it.

That is what is meant by "double taxation" of corporations.

However, there is a provision in the Internal Revenue Code that allows a C Corp to elect to be taxed as a Subchapter S Corporation, which is still a C Corp but is taxed differently.

Subchapter S is a subchapter of the Tax Code covering corporations.

It is actually U.S. Code > Title 26 > Internal Revenue Code > Subtitle A > Income Taxes > Chapter 1 > Normal Taxes and Surtaxes > Subchapter S > Tax Treatment of S Corporations and Their Shareholders. It's a real hoot.

The difference is that the S Corporation does not pay taxes at the corporate level. The corporation reports the income and expenses at the corporate level on Form 1120S, but the income, deductions, credits and other items drop through to the shareholders on Schedule K-1 to be reported on their personal tax returns.

So, an S Corp is just a C Corp that has elected to be taxed differently.

Now, back to the LLC that you formed.

And more IRS logic.

As I said, Form 8832 allows the LLC to elect to be taxed either as a Partnership or as a Corporation. But if you choose to be taxed as a Corporation, it would be a C Corp, and you don't want that.

So, after you file Form 8832 electing to taxed as a C Corp, you must then file Form 2553 Election by a Small Business Corporation, choosing S Corp status.

However (are you still with me?), the IRS has decided that you can also just file Form 2553 without first filing Form 8832, and your LLC will be treated for tax purposes as an S Corp.

So you can create your LLC, not file Form 8832 and be in the default status of Disregarded Entity, and then file Form 2553 electing to be taxed as an S Corp even though you have not first elected to become a "Small Business Corporation."

Anyway, it works. The IRS has been faithful in allowing S Corp status for LLCs that just file Form 2553.

You make your own decision.

Personally, I file Form 8832 and then file Form 2553.

Now, back to the reason that you are doing this.

Two things to note.

1.)   S Corp income is not considered Self-Employment Income and is not subject to the 15.3% Self-Employment Tax. This is something that you would want.

2.) The owner of an S Corp who is managing the business is required to pay himself what the IRS considers a reasonable salary.

The definition of "reasonable salary" is not provided by the IRS, and there are no calculations to determine the amount. Obviously, if the business earns all of its income from the services provided by the owner, such as an outside sales company, a reasonable salary would be virtually all of the income, because the owner "is the company."

It's a crap shoot. You pick a number and the IRS decides whether or not you got it right.

But for a Hard Money Lender, your efforts are only one part of production of income. The funds and the business operation account for a significant portion.

If your annual Gross Income of $72,000 is reduced by operating expenses to a Net Operating Income of $62,000, you would probably be safe with paying yourself a salary of $20,000, considering the amount of time you are spending and the number of loans per month that are being made.

This would mean that $42,000 of Net Income from the S Corp would drop through to you as taxable income, but not as Self-Employment Income, and therefore not subject to the additional 15.3% Self-Employment Tax.

You would save $6,426 in taxes.

This is the primary reason for choosing to have your LLC taxed as an S Corp.

BUSINESS MODEL

At the beginning of this Chapter, in Overview, I described briefly what your Business Model will look like.

Now I will provide more detail, and break it down into:

1.) The Deal.

2.) The Borrower.

3.) The Property.

4.) The Loan.

THE DEAL

Your success as a Hard Money Lender will depend on the three things that you provide to the Borrower that no other Lender can provide.

1.) You have the cash, and it is available now.

2.) You can qualify the Borrower and approve the loan with minimum paperwork.

3.) You can be ready to fund the loan in a matter of days, not weeks or months.

This is why you are able to charge very high interest rates.

It is not a situation where the Borrower can't get a loan anywhere else.

He just can't get this particular loan quickly and with a minimum of qualification anywhere else.

The primary service provided by the Hard Money Lender is speed. For example, if the kitchen upgrade is finished this afternoon, you can inspect the work, take pictures of it, scan the receipts, and write the next check for the bathroom and the roof, all within a couple of hours, and the Borrower can be picking up the material at Lowe's the next morning.

No other Lender can do that. And that's why you have the business.

You should always control all of the elements of the loan, the amount, the interest rate, the points, and the duration.

This is one of the unique characteristics of Hard Money Lending, and one of the strongest reasons for going into it.

With other types of investments, you don't know the Profit or the ROI until you are well into it, and maybe not until the end.

But with Hard Money Lending, you know it at the beginning. In fact, you decide what you want your Profit or ROI to be, and that is the only way you are willing to structure the loan. If the Borrower does not want to pay the 12%, you just hold your cash, and talk to the next Borrower.

You will usually discover that if the Borrower thinks that $6,000 is too much to pay for the use of your money for 6 months to buy **and** rehab a property, the project is probably not a very good one, or he is not the one who should be doing it.

If you fail to manage your business very tightly, sticking to your strict guidelines, and you end up with six loans, all of different amounts, all with different interest rates and different points, and all maturing at irregular intervals, then trying to manage your company will be a living Hell.

Remember, this is your business.

You want $50,000 going out each month, and a different $50,000 coming back in each month, and Gross Income of $6,000 each month.

If you don't have a system like this, you will never know where you are, so you won't be able to plan where you are going, or how to get there, and you won't be able to increase your volume to increase your income, when you think the time is right to do so.

It's your money, your business, and your system.

Manage it like a Business Manager.

THE BORROWER

Selecting the right Borrower will be the key to your success.

Your first choice is a Borrower who is experienced in the process of using hard money, and has done the same thing a number of times before.

Ideally, he will also be the Contractor and will be doing the work.

He will probably already have the package of information together when he first comes to you.

You can tell by looking at his Statement of Work (SOW) whether he is a good risk. If it is very specific and shows a knowledge of material and labor costs, and the construction business, then he is probably someone you want to have as a Borrower.

Of course, this requires that you have a certain amount of knowledge yourself regarding residential construction, or at least rehab experience. If you do not have this, you should know someone that you can take the documents to and get an opinion. I have found that the older male employees at Lowe's and Home Depot are likely to have the expertise that you need. I hired one to help me look at completed work and materials lists on a "pier and beam" project because I had never done one, and he saved me about ten times what I paid him, maybe more. There is a Hell of a lot of difference between a 2X6 and a 2X8 in a foundation.

In this same vein, one of the things that you will require from your Borrower is a Broker's Price Opinion (BPO) regarding the probable Fair Market Value (FMV) of the property after the rehab is completed, also called the After Repair Value (ARV).

You should also get your own BPO, from a different Broker, of course, and then compare the two documents. In addition to educating yourself about real estate values in the specific area at the time, this will also give you insight to the two Brokers who did the opinions, and probably into the Borrower, depending on how the two BPOs compare.

You might also want to run a Credit Report on the Borrower.

But be aware that the Credit Report might not contain any private loans that he has outstanding, such as the one you are considering extending to him.

But the Credit Report will tell you almost everything else about his financial situation, and this will be beneficial information for you to know if you have a professional business relationship with him.

THE PROPERTY

You should have a fair amount of knowledge about the real property in the area where you intend to do business.

After all, you are in the real estate business.

The BPO that the Borrower provides you, and the one that you get yourself, will tell you the basic information about the property, as well as two opinions about it.

You should also inspect the property and take photos.

When you are starting out, you might want to take the Statement of Work (SOW) provided to you by the Borrower, and pay a local Contractor a couple of hundred dollars to walk through the property with you and give his opinion.

You will learn a lot about the property, about the Borrower, and about how to do this yourself on the next deal.

THE LOAN

Loans are based primarily on the value of the property instead of the credit of the Borrower.

Bank loans are based on the customer credit history. Hard Money Loans are based on the deal.

The total amount of the loan is never more than 65% of the ARV. In the best case, it will only be 50%.

Hard Money Loans are asset-based lending, but with some amount of Borrower qualification.

The experience, skill and character of the Borrower is important, but a Newbie with a great deal can also turn out well.

The Borrower likes Hard Money Lending because he knows that he is talking directly to the person who will make the decision and who will write the check, instead of a bank employee who has been told what to say to everyone and has no decision-making authority, and he likes that. You should point this out whenever the opportunity arises. Always remember that he is paying top dollar for your services.

And your services need to be quick and professional.

LEGAL DOCUMENTS

Even before you get to the legal documents necessary for the loan, the legal document that you should look at, prior to approving the loan or even taking the Loan Application, is the Purchase Agreement that the Borrower has signed with the property owner.

Unfortunately, many Real Estate Investors do not realize how important the Purchase Agreement is, and so they do a sloppy job of filling it out and getting it signed.

But it is a Contract, and if it isn't done so that it is legally binding, you will be wasting a lot of time and some money with a deal that might not close.

You should look at the Purchase Agreement carefully and make sure that it is correct. If you don't know enough to make that determination, take it to an Attorney, preferably one that works for a Title Company, and have him tell you if it has problems.

If it needs to be amended, you should have the Borrower do that before you take his Loan Application.

The first legal document, after the Purchase Agreement, will be a Loan Agreement, between you and the Borrower, stipulating the terms of your agreement. It will not become part of the transaction or part of the real estate closing. It is just between you and the Borrower, but it is very important. It will contain the Borrower's agreement to pay for the cost of your legal documents, for instance, and his agreement that you will hold the construction funds in escrow and dispense them in stages, following inspection and approval of the work.

It will also contain his agreement to personally guarantee the loan, although you will have a separate document for him to sign at Closing for this.

The entire business agreement between you and the Borrower should be contained in your Loan Agreement.

The legal documents that you will need for Closing will be a Real Estate Lien Note and a Deed of Trust, or the equivalent in your State.

The Real Estate Lien Note contains all of the information about the Loan, the manner in which it will be paid, and a description of what constitutes a Default.

The Deed of Trust will appoint a person or entity to act as a Trustee, the person who will Foreclose on the property in the event of default.

You should have your Attorney prepare the Real Estate Lien Note and Deed of Trust, and make them available to the Title Company ahead of time, because the Title Company will be arranging to have the other documents between the Buyer and Seller prepared by another Attorney.

One of these other documents, the Warranty Deed With Vendor's Lien, will reference your Real Estate Lien Note and Deed of Trust, so they must be available ahead of time, as soon as you know the Closing Date.

You should also require that the property have a casualty insurance policy with you, the Hard Money Lender, named as Loss Payee. This will not be prepared prior to Closing, but the Insurance Agent should provide a Binder that will be given to you at Closing.

You should require a Personal Guaranty on every loan, especially when you are making a loan to an LLC. You can loan to an LLC even though most Lenders will not, because you have the Personal Guaranty of the Borrower.

You should also have your Attorney prepare the Personal Guaranty because there are many different kinds, and you want to make sure that yours fits your situation instead of just have the Title Company fill out a form.

CLOSING

Assuming that a Title Company is doing the Closing, you will have nothing to do.

You are entitled to attend, and I recommend that you do so. You will be able to sit at the table and learn exactly what takes place, and this will enhance your education.

Prior to the Closing date, you will provide the Title Company with the financing documents, the Real Estate Note and Deed of Trust. You will also provide them with any other documents that you want signed as part of the transaction, such as the Personal Guaranty.

Also, prior to the Closing, you will provide the Title Company with the Loan Proceeds. In the example we are using, that would be $50,000. You can drop off a Cashiers Check, or you can wire the funds to the Title Company's bank account.

As a Lender, you are entitled to present the Title Company with a set of Closing Instructions, telling them exactly how you insist that everything be done in order to protect your funds, but I would recommend that you only communicate specific items to them personally, such as the signing of the Personal Guaranty, or cutting the check for the Construction Funds back to you.

I was a Title Company Closer for many years, and I always found it insulting to be instructed how to do my job by someone who didn't know what they were talking about, just because they had the money to fund the deal, and felt that they could use threats to run everything.

It is not a good way to make friends. And there are a lot of things the Closer can do, or not do, without breaking any rules, that will not be in your best interest.

Treat the Title Company Closer like a professional, and you are likely to be treated the same.

You will be provided a copy of the Closing Documents that pertain to you, in advance, and also a copy of the Closing Statement, once called a HUD-1, and now called various things, but still referred to as a HUD-1.

You might notice on the Closing Statement that your Borrower is being given some money that you didn't know about.

This is because property taxes accrue daily throughout the year, so there will be some amount due and unpaid at the time of Closing. The annual amount will be prorated and the accrued liability will be taken from the Seller's funds and credited to the Buyer's funds, because he will have to pay the property taxes at the end of the year.

Be aware of this and make sure that he does pay the property taxes, if your loan period extends through the end of the year.

FUNDING AND INSPECTION

At the Closing, in addition to receiving a signed copy of your Real Estate Lien Note, and a copy of your signed Deed of Trust, you should receive, in our example, a check for $20,000 identified as "Construction Draw" or whatever you instruct the Closer to call it.

After the Closing, you should look at the Statement of Work (SOW) provided you by your Borrower and agree with him on which work he will do first, and on the amount of funds he will need. Then you write him a check for that amount.

You should inspect the progress of the work on an irregular basis, not on the same day every week. Do random inspections. Take photos. You can refer to these in order to document the progress.

When the Borrower tells you that one of the phases is complete, you visit, take photos, inspect the work, copy or photo the receipts showing that the money advanced has been used for its intended purpose, and write a check for the next phase.

Once you have disbursed all of the construction funds, and inspected the last of the work, meet with the Borrower and discuss how he intends to proceed.

He might decide to refinance the project and keep the property, or he might decide to list it and sell it. You need to know what is supposed to be happening so that you can monitor it.

FORECLOSURE

In a very high percentage of the cases, the Loan will be repaid on time.

In some cases, you might have to extend the loan period under the conditions set out in the Real Estate Lien Note.

And in some few cases, the Borrower, for whatever reason, will not be able to pay the loan as promised, and the loan will go into default.

Default usually just leads to the property being deeded to the HML.

There is a specific legal document for this, called a "Deed In Lieu Of Foreclosure." As it sounds, the Borrower deeds the property to the Lender in order to not have the property foreclosed on and have the foreclosure on the Borrower's credit record.

It is usually a friendly situation.

The Borrower usually has other problems and is glad to get this property off his plate so that he can deal with the other matters.

The Hard Money Lender is usually satisfied to be deeded a property worth maybe $100,000 and for which he has only put out $50,000 plus a couple of thousand in expenses and fees.

For the Hard Money Lender, there are two aspects of "the value of the property." One is the value of the property in the condition when it was purchased, and the other is the After Repair Value (ARV).

Make sure that you can at least break even if you have to foreclose on the property the day after the loan is made because the Borrower disappeared. Once the property is in the process of being rehabbed, you will almost always be assured that there is more value in the property than what you have invested.

If Foreclosure does become necessary, there will be certain steps that you must take when the six-month loan period is expired, and the Borrower cannot pay the loan.

The Hard Money Loan will usually contain a "grace period" because the future is unpredictable.

Your Real Estate Lien Note will have a Due Date, of course, but it will also contain a provision whereby you can decide to allow a "grace period" in your sole discretion, with the terms and conditions stipulated.

For instance, you might have the option of charging a $500 penalty for the first 30-day extension, along with a daily interest accrual amount. For a second 30-day extension, you might charge a $1,000 penalty plus the same daily interest accrual amount or a higher amount.

Of course, you can also start the foreclosure process immediately instead of granting an extension, and the interest will continue to accrue at the same rate as the daily accrual amount during the term of the note.

Or, depending on the law in your State, you might be able to do both, start the Foreclosure and also extend the loan, and then cancel the Foreclosure if the loan extension works out, and foreclose if it does not.

Your method of Foreclosure will depend on the law of the State in which you are operating.

In those States with non-judicial foreclosure laws, the Trustee named in the Deed of Trust posts a Notice on the Public Bulletin Board at the Courthouse of the County in which the property is located, and on a stipulated day of the month a certain period of time in the future, the Trustee will sell the property on the steps of the Courthouse.

You will need to learn the laws governing Foreclosure for the State where you intend to do business.

PAYOFF

If the project goes as planned, your Borrower will either refinance the property from your loan into a permanent loan, and there will be a Closing at the Title Company, where the debts against the property are paid off and a new lien created in favor of the new Lender, or sell the property, which will also produce a payoff.

One of the debts that will be paid off is your Loan.

You will provide the Title Company with a Payoff Amount.

You will be required to attend the Closing because when you are handed your check, you will be required to sign a document that will be called something like "Release of Deed of Trust Lien," or just "Release of Lien."

You might also be required to surrender the original Real Estate Lien Note, marked as paid, but probably not.

MANAGING YOUR BUSINESS

One of the best aspects of Hard Money Lending as a method of Real Estate Investing is that you are totally in control of how much you want to do.

TIME REQUIRED

The time required to establish yourself in the business will depend on how big you want your operation to be.

If you intend to be a one-man operation, it can be done in a minimum amount of time.

If you intend to have an office, with a Secretary or Personal Assistant, and a website, the time could amount to what it would be to start any other business, such as a Property Management business.

But most Hard Money Lenders start out as an individual, with money to loan, and a reasonable amount of knowledge about Real Estate Investing, and some knowledge of construction.

In this case, you proceed at your own pace, making yourself known to everyone involved with real estate sales, with other lenders, including the Bank Loan Officers. Then you visit construction sites, and make as many contacts as you can.

You need to have a goal before you start.

Do you want to do one $50,000 loan per month, or two?

Determining what you want to do will determine how much time is required.

SKILLS REQUIRED

As you can tell by reading the material up to this point, you should have some knowledge of Real Estate Investing.

If you do not, you should have someone you can rely on temporarily, and have a plan for learning what you need to know very quickly.

There are successful Hard Money Lenders who started without this knowledge, so don't be discouraged.

You will constantly be learning and adjusting, and paying a price for your mistakes and lack of knowledge. But that would be true of almost any business.

If this is something you think you would enjoy, then you should do it, because the learning process will also be enjoyable.

And the ROI is better than almost anything else you could be doing.

And remember, you are totally in control of your life.

MONEY REQUIRED

Money is the name of the game.

You gotta have it to make it.

This is not one of those areas of Real Estate Investing where you can expect to get rich starting out with nothing, assuming there are any of those.

Start with the money you have. If it is only $20,000 then find the Mobile Home investors in your area. Read

Chapter 7 to learn about Mobile Home Investing. Some of those deals return around 90%, so they would be happy to pay your interest rate.

If you are fortunate enough to have your own funds, the amount required will depend on how much income you want.

As I demonstrated earlier, $300,000 would be a reasonable amount to build a good business.

If you are charging ten percent plus two points for a six-month loan of $50,000 and you are only doing one loan a month, then your annual Gross Income will be $72,000.

Assuming a monthly overhead and loan cost of $1,000 that will result in an annual income of $60,000.

Determine the annual income you would like, multiply it by five, and you have the amount of money required to run a business like this.

LIABILITY

As a Hard Money Lender you will have no personal liability for anything that happens regarding the property that secures your loan.

If the property, or the property owner, incurs a liability, and it leads to a judgment, and therefore to a lien on the property, you still will not have a concern.

Your loan will be a lien that is classified as a "purchase money lien" and therefore it will have priority for payoff over any other lien on the property, in case the property should have to be sold to satisfy a judgment.

None of the potential liability of the project will attach to you.

As to the liability that you might have for operating your business, there are the normal liabilities for similar businesses. For the loan business, there are laws called Usury Laws.

These are both State and Federal Laws, and they limit the amount of interest that can be charged on loans. Mostly they cover consumer loans, and personal loans. But there are some restrictions on commercial loans.

Find out what the limits are for the State in which you are operating and follow them. This is another reason to have a good Attorney who understands this area of the law to draft your Real Estate Lien Note and other financing documents.

There are even some States where language can be put into the documents that says that if it turns out that the amount of interest being charged is in violation of the law, then the parties agree that the remedy will be to adjust the rate of interest to "the highest amount permitted by law" and refund any overpayment.

As I said before, a good Attorney will be one of the best expenses you will have.

TAXATION

Taxation of your income will be determined by whether you are operating as an individual or as a business entity.

I strongly recommend that you form an LLC and elect to have that LLC taxed as an S Corp.

On the Federal level, the S Corp will file a Form 1120S tax return, but will not pay federal taxes. Instead, the S Corp will send a Schedule K-1 to the owner of the S Corp that shows the income, deductions, credits and other items which will be reported on Schedule E of the owner's personal tax return.

Some of the States treat the S Corp differently than the Federal government, so you need to find out what the situation is in the State where you intend to operate.

CONCLUSION

Real Estate Investing offers some of the highest ROIs of any business.

It's almost at the level of wealth-accumulation during the Oil and Gas Boom in the Southwest, and the Gold Rush in California.

And like those, it is "entrepreneur-driven," meaning that it is fueled by individual effort.

Anyone who is willing to learn the process and do the work can be successful.

But not all of them have the necessary resources, and the main resource required, after knowledge, is money.

This is where the Hard Money Lender comes in.

The HML is like the Retail Merchant who sold or rented equipment to the Wildcatters and the Gold Prospectors.

They had to have the equipment, and their potential ROI was so high that they were willing to pay a premium for it. Other than a Claim or a Drilling Lease, it was their total investment.

Sometimes the Wildcatters and the Prospectors made money, and sometimes they didn't.

But the Retail Merchant always made money. Usually a lot.

And so will the Hard Money Lender.

The Hard Money Lender will not only make a high ROI with very low risk, but the time requirement can be anything that he wants, depending on how much total income he wants to make, and how much money he has.

As I said, it is my favorite of the Ten Real Estate Investments.

Good Luck!

CHAPTER 2

PRIVATE LENDING

OVERVIEW

The Private Money Lender operates in the space between the Hard Money Lender and the Bank.

The Hard Money Lender will be loaning for the short term, usually six months, and the Borrower will usually be buying a property to rehab. The Bank, on the other hand, will be creating Mortgages, usually for 15, 20, 25, or 30 years, although there might be a Balloon Payment at some point, after three years or five years.

The Private Money Lender, referred to as a PML, will be making loans for the period in between, usually for one year to five years.

This market is not subject to competition from the Hard Money Lender because he doesn't want to tie up funds for that long, and the market is not subject to competition from the Bank because the Bank does not want to loan for such a short term.

The Borrower in this mid-term lending market is the Real Estate Investor who plans to buy a property and hold it for a specified term, and then exit. He is a Buy And Hold investor, but not a long-term investor.

The Borrower is willing to pay a higher interest rate because the Private Money Lender is easier to deal with, the qualifications are easier, and the transaction is quicker and less complicated. And remember, Banks just don't want to do these loans, even if the Borrower qualifies, which many do not.

The interest rate is usually in the 7-10% range, with no points involved.

The Private Money Lender is willing to make these loans because he usually has funds that are invested elsewhere and earning about 2%.

The Private Money Lender is not the Commercial Lender, who is in direct competition with the Bank for large, long-term, financing of Apartment Buildings and Shopping Centers.

Private Money Lending is very similar to Note Investing, except that the investor is creating his own Note instead of buying an existing Note.

Now, let's break this down and look at the normal elements of Real Estate Investing and see how each of the elements works for Private Money Lending.

Those elements are:

1.) Income.

2.) Expenses.

3.) Cash Flow.

4.) Appreciation.

5.) Leverage.

6.) Tax Advantages.

They are the same as they were for the prior Chapter on Hard Money Lending, and some of the information will be the same. If you have not read Chapter 1 yet, you should stop and do that now.

INCOME

The income from Private Money Lending will be the interest earned on the money that was loaned. Simple.

The loan amounts generally range from $50,000 to $300,000.

For an Example, we will use $100,000 at 7% for 5 years.

This means that each month, the Private Money Lender will receive a monthly payment of $1,980.12.

For the first monthly payment, of this amount, $583.33 would represent the accrued Interest on the loan, and $1,396.79 would represent the repayment of Principal.

But for the second monthly payment, the Interest income would be $575.19 and the return of Principal would be $1,404.93.

So, you can see, your income from this investment would be different each month if you elect to amortize the loan over the 60-month payback period.

For the last payment, the Interest income would only be $11.48.

If you amortize the loan, with monthly payments of Principal and Interest, the total interest received in five years would be $18,807.22.

If your purpose for becoming a Private Money Lender is to create a stream of interest income from a pool of funds, you will probably want to draft the Real Estate Lien Note so that payments are interest-only, and then the entire Principal is payable at the end of five years.

With this arrangement, your monthly payments would be annual Interest amount of $7,000 divided by 12 months, which is $583.33.

Over the five-year term of the loan your total Interest income would be $35,000 instead of $18,807.22.

Keep in mind, the purpose of Private Money Lending is to keep your funds earning interest for you. If you amortize the Note, your total interest income for the first 12 months will be $6,451.66, which is only 6.45%, not 7.0%. The remainder of each payment is just you getting your money back. It is no longer earning interest income for you, and the amount that you get back is not large enough to loan it out again.

If you do not want to tie up your funds for five years, you could make the Note interest-only for each monthly payment, and then annual payments of one-fifth of the amount of the Loan. The $20,000 that you get back might be enough to make another Loan, and keep your funds earning income.

If you would like to run your own Amortization Schedule and play around with the numbers, a very good resource is: https://www.mortgagecalculator.org/calcs/amortization.php

And if you would like to learn about the Calculations that Real Estate Investors use to make their decisions, I have a book on Amazon called "50 Real Estate Investing Calculations" at amazon.com/dp/B077ZRNZKN.

EXPENSES

You will have the regular expenses of operating any business, which will depend on how much you want to be involved in Private Money Lending.

But other than the basic office expenses, your expenses for Private Money Lending investing will include the cost of an Attorney, since the legal documents will be the primary tools of your trade.

You can read about the expenses of being a Hard Money Lender in the previous Chapter, and adapt those to what you want to do with Private Money Lending.

CASH FLOW

Your cash flow will basically be your Interest income earned on the loan.

If you amortize the loan, and receive monthly payments of both principal and interest, the amount of "cash" that is "flowing" will be more, but most of it will just be your own money coming back.

APPRECIATION

Appreciation does not figure into the decision or calculation, except that the real estate that is securing your loan will probably appreciate in value over the five year term of the loan, and therefore your security will be getting better as you go.

LEVERAGE

See the discussion in the previous Chapter on Hard Money Lending. The same information applies here.

TAX ADVANTAGES

There are no tax advantages like the ones that are available to the Real Estate Investor who is owning rental real estate.

BUSINESS ENTITY

Read about business entities in Chapter 1 – Hard Money Lending. The same information applies here.

BUSINESS MODEL

The Private Money Lending Business Model can be divided into the following parts for analysis.

1.) The Deal.

2.) The Borrower.

3.) The Property.

4.) The Loan.

THE DEAL

A Bank will spend the same amount of time and resources to create a 30-year loan as it will spend on a three-year or five-year loan. So, the costs for the shorter-term loan will be just as high for the Borrower, and the qualifications will be just as stringent.

And a Bank really does not want to do these short-term loans.

So, the market is wide open to the Private Money Lender.

The Private Money Lender will loan for a period of one to five years, at an interest rate that is higher than the Bank's rate, and might even charge a couple of points.

Where the Hard Money Lending is mostly an asset-based loan, Private Money Lending is primarily a relationship-based loan. The property will usually be an established rental property with a known, or knowable, Fair Market Value (FMV), and if you loan 70% of the FMV you will be fairly safe unless the asset loses at least a third of its value.

And a little known fact of financing is that in many States the financing documents allow the Lender to foreclose on a property if the FMV of the property falls below the amount owed on the loan, unless the Borrower pays down the loan principal.

The Private Money Lender will usually be loaning to a business entity, which will probably be an LLC, and so it will be acceptable to require a Personal Guaranty from the owner of the LLC. In the event that Foreclosure becomes necessary, the individual will usually just deed the property to the Lender rather than end up with a judgment and ruined credit.

The Private Money Lender who runs an efficient and professional operation will often have the same Borrower requesting additional loans, and will also have people approaching him to become involved in his business as investors. It is a very likely prelude to the larger business of Syndication.

One word of caution: make sure that the Borrower has a plan for "forced appreciation" of the property, other than just Buy And Hold. The real estate market goes down as well as up.

And you might even require copies of the monthly Profit and Loss Statement, and a yearly inspection of the property. The amount of involvement you choose to have will depend on the stability of the project.

THE BORROWER

The Borrower for Private Money Lending cannot be as easily identified as the Borrower for the Hard Money Lender. The Hard Money Lender's Borrowers are almost always finding a distressed property, buying it, rehabbing it, and either flipping it or going into permanent financing and holding it.

The Borrower for the Private Money Lender can be doing any number of things.

The Borrower might just be new to the area, and the Banks do not want to deal with him until he becomes established.

These loans are classified as Commercial Loans and Banks prefer to deal with established businesses on Commercial Loans, not a new business.

Banks loan on credit history, but the Private Money Lender will look at the individual and listen to his reasons why he is a good loan risk.

He might be someone who just found another Duplex like the one he already has, at a good price, and knows he can keep it rented because he already has a waiting list, and he has the knowledge and experience to manage it. His plan is to stabilize the income, do some cosmetic work over the short-term, and sell it to a new investor. He doesn't want a 30-year Mortgage, and he doesn't want the aggravation of dealing with a Bank. The Private Money Lender is perfect for him.

Or, if you are lending larger sums, your Borrower might be someone who finds small apartment buildings that are somewhat rundown, cleans them up, stabilizes the rental income, and either sells them on, or gets a new appraisal and refinances and takes out cash.

If you are lending for shorter periods of time, your Borrower might be a purchaser of Mobile Homes, where the notes typically have a 24-month to 36-month payback.

The Private Money Lender has a large group of Borrowers who need funding for a period of one to five years, and are willing to pay a premium interest rate.

THE PROPERTY

The property involved in Private Money Lending

is as varied as the Borrowers will be varied, but your process of securing your loan will be the same for each.

You should take the same basic steps regarding the property that are taken by the Hard Money Lender.

Please review the prior Chapter.

THE LOAN

The Private Money Lender is essentially operating as a Bank.

The difference is that the loan is for a shorter period of time, he can make all of the rules because he is not subject to Federal or State banking regulations, and he is dealing with one-year to five-year paybacks instead of 30-year mortgages.

LEGAL DOCUMENTS

The legal documents that you will use are the same ones that would be used by a Bank in a similar financing transaction for a Mortgage.

The only difference is that the terms will be shorter.

If the Borrower already owns the property, the documents will be a Real Estate Lien Note and a Deed of Trust, or the equivalent in your State.

If the Borrower is purchasing the property, then there will also be a Deed involved.

Like the Hard Money Lender, you will need a good Attorney, and I refer you to the information in the prior Chapter about making the decision concerning an Attorney.

CLOSING

If your Borrower is purchasing property, then the Closing will be arranged by the Buyer and Seller, or their representatives, and your only involvement will be to provide the funding and to provide the legal documents that you require to be signed.

You may or may not be required to be present at the Closing, but I recommend that you attend, and benefit from the additional experience.

In addition, you can make sure that your documents are signed correctly, and answer any questions at the closing table about the documents or the financing.

You will also want to pick up the Insurance Binder on the property that shows you as the Loss Payee.

FUNDING AND INSPECTION

You should inspect the property before you fund the loan.

The process should be very similar to the steps taken by the Hard Money Lender.

The funding will be done when you are notified of the Closing date, and you will turn your funds over to the Title Company and they will handle everything, file the documents in the county records, and provide you with copies.

FORECLOSURE

Most Private Money Loans do not involve a risk of foreclosure.

The property is usually well established, and is already producing income, with very little speculative nature to it.

In the rare event that the Borrower suffers personal difficulties, or the market in general declines, you will probably just have the property deeded to you rather than having to go through the foreclosure process.

Foreclosure laws are different for every State, and you should make yourself familiar with what they are in your State.

PAYOFF

As I explained earlier, you can amortize your loan over the life and receive monthly payments that will be part interest and part return of principal.

In this case your interest income will decline each month, and the amount of the principal returned will not really be enough to do anything with in the way of creating more income.

So, most Private Money Lenders prefer to have the monthly payments be interest-only so that they will remain at the same high amount, and then have periodic lump sum principal payments, or have the entire principal returned when the loan is paid off, so that it is then available for another loan.

But one of the great things about Private Money Lending is that, unlike the Bank, you can write any terms that you want into the loan.

You can have interest paid monthly, quarterly, or annually.

You can have principal repayments periodically in specified amounts.

You can have a fixed-rate note or an adjustable-rate note.

This is really all about how you want to use your money to receive the most benefit.

MANAGING YOUR BUSINESS

Of all of the Ten Other Real Estate Investments, the Private Money Lending model probably requires the least amount of time and commitment.

TIME REQUIRED

Once the loan is funded, there might be nothing else for you to do for five years.

At least, not on that loan.

But you will probably want to be doing a number of these loans, because you will probably be contacted by people who would like to loan you money at above the 2% they are getting with their CDs, so that you can then make loans with the funds.

The time required to be a Private Money Lender will be determined by just how much you want to do.

SKILLS REQUIRED

There's no getting around it.

This is Real Estate Finance 101.

You have to know it, or you have to learn it.

I think you will enjoy it, but then my degree is in Finance. I enjoyed it so much that I completed the hours necessary for an Accounting degree and then did the fourth year courses in Finance.

So, other than the necessary "people skills" that you will need, knowledge of finance, and familiarity with Real Estate Law would serve you well.

MONEY REQUIRED

It's all about money.

If you plan to loan it, you must have it.

Once you have a few performing loans, say $50,000 to $100,000 each, you will have people wanting you to loan out their money, or borrow it yourself at maybe 5%, which is probably twice what they are now earning.

The problem with using other people's money is that the float will only be 2-5%, hardly enough to justify the time and risk unless you are talking about $300,000 and up.

The real purpose of Private Money Lending is to change your own investment portfolio from earning 2-3% to earning 7-8%, and more.

LIABILITY

See the prior Chapter on Hard Money Lending for a discussion of Liability.

TAXATION

Taxation of your income will be determined by whether you are operating as an individual or as a business entity.

I strongly recommend that you form an LLC and elect to have that LLC taxed as an S Corp.

On the Federal level, the S Corp will file a Form 1120S tax return, but will not pay federal taxes. Instead, the S Corp will send a Schedule K-1 to the owner of the S Corp that shows the income, deductions, credits and other items which will be reported on Schedule E of the owner's personal tax return.

Some of the States treat the S Corp differently than the Federal government, so you need to find out what the situation is in the State where you intend to operate.

CONCLUSION

Private Money Lending is a safe type of investment that requires little of your time and provides you with almost complete control of your activities.

Your investments will be for a one to five year period, and you will control all of the terms of the investment.

Once you have created a few performing loans, you will probably be approached by people who want to take part in your business in some way, or loan you their own funds for you to use.

CHAPTER 3

NOTES

OVERVIEW

The term "Note Investing" is often used incorrectly to refer to a number of situations and activities that do not actually constitute Note Investing.

Note Investing is the act of buying a Real Estate Lien Note.

That's it.

The money you pay for the Note is the investment.

The Note Payments that you receive are the returns on your investment.

For example, there is a $100,000 Note with an interest rate of 7%, a term of 5 years, and a monthly payment of $1,980.12. It is secured by a Single Family Residence (SFR) with a Fair Market Value (FMV) of $135,000.

The Real Estate Lien Note is one year old and the remaining principal balance is $82,690.22 and all payments are current.

The Owner of the Note needs funds for a new investment, and he offers to sell you the note for $70,000 cash.

It sounds to you like a safe investment, but you want to know your ROI. You know it will be more than 7% since you bought the Note at a discount.

So, you crank up your Amortization Calculator and plug in $70,000 as the Loan Amount, 4 years as the Term (# of payments remaining), and $1980.12 as the Payment, and tap the Interest button.

Your Interest Rate, as the ROI, calculates to be 15.89%.

This is Note Investing.

If you would like to test this for yourself, go to:

https://www.mortgagecalculator.org/calcs/amortization.php

And if you would like to know more about Calculations like this that are used in Real Estate Investing, I have a book on Amazon entitled "50 Real Estate Investing Calculations: Cash Flow, IRR, Value, Profit, Equity, Income, ROI, Depreciation, More: With Links To The 24 Best Calculators."

You can find it at:

Amazon.com/Michael-Lantrip/e/B01N2ZRGUY.

WHAT IS A NOTE

The Note that we will be talking about is a Real Estate Lien Note, or it might be called something differently in your location, but we will just call it a Note.

A Note is a promise by an individual or legal entity to make specified periodic payments of a designated amount on a certain date for a certain period of time to a named individual or entity.

For example, John Smith promises to pay $1,980.12 to Bob Baker on the 10th day of each month for five years, for a total of 60 payments.

This is the legal obligation contained in the Note.

The Note will be secured by a first lien on real estate that is described on another document called a Deed of Trust, which empowers the Trustee named in that document to foreclose on the real estate in the event of Default.

The names of these documents and the rules for foreclosure will vary for each State and you will need to learn what these are for your State (I capitalize State here for purposes of clarity, and, yes, it is proper to do so under the rules of Grammar).

There are many different types of Notes, depending on the circumstances under which they were created.

A Purchase Money Note is created when money is loaned for the purchase of the real estate.

There are First Lien Notes and Second Lien Notes.

There are Interest-Only Notes.

There are many other types of Notes.

The Note we will be discussing is a First Lien Note that is either a Purchase Money Note or a refinance of a Purchase Money Note.

WHERE TO FIND NOTES

There is no marketplace for the types of Notes that we are talking about.

Banks will usually have a Department, or at least one Officer, who deals in selling Real Estate Lien Notes that the Bank wants to get off its books, but these are also not the types of Notes that we are interested in. These Notes are usually delinquent, or "non-performing," meaning that payments have not been made for at least 90 days.

So, unless you are an Attorney and can do all of the legal work yourself, you do not want to buy Second Lien Notes, nor Delinquent Notes, nor unsecured Notes.

OK, so where are the Notes and how do you find them?

The Notes will usually be held by Real Estate Investors, and by individuals who have done Seller Financing when they sold a property.

The first thing that you need to do is to make yourself known, and make your interest in buying Notes known, by going around and establishing contact with everyone with any connection to the real estate community.

You should establish and maintain contact with:

1.) Bank Loan Officers,

2.) Every employee and every Sales Agent in every Realtor office in your area,

3.) Every Insurance Salesman,

4.) All of the employees of every Title Company in your area,

5.) All local Attorneys, and

6.) All local Accountants and Bookkeepers.

You should also run a small display ad at least weekly in the Real Estate section of the local newspaper, saying something simple like "I Buy Notes."

While you are waiting for someone to contact you, there is something else you can do that I have found to be very productive.

It involves you finding the Note holder, instead of waiting for the Note holder to find you.

Learn how to search the Real Estate records of your County Courthouse.

Then understand this.

When an owner of real estate sells a property and does Seller Financing, a Deed is filed on that property in the Real Estate Records of the County where the property is located. Actually, it is probably called something like a Warranty Deed With Vendor's Lien.

There is also a Real Estate Lien Note signed by the buyer of the property, but it will not be "filed of record."

However, the other document that will be filed of record is the document that creates the lien on the property that will secure the Real Estate Lien Note. It will probably be called either a Deed of Trust, or a Mortgage, depending on which State you live in.

The Deed and the lien document will be dated the same day, and will be filed on the same day.

So, you search the Deed Records, which will probably be combined with the "lien records" and you will identify the individuals who have sold property and done Seller Financing.

They are holding Notes.

Start with the records for about two years ago, because you want to buy a Note that has a history of about two years of payments.

A second way to find Notes is one that few people know about, and one that I have found to be almost a sure thing.

Search the Real Estate records and find the documents where a lien on real estate has been transferred from an individual to a Lender, usually a Bank. It will be called something like a Transfer of Lien, or Assignment of Lien.

Read the document and see if the lien that the person transferred is one that the person received when he sold a property.

If it is, here's what happened. The person probably sold real estate and did Seller Financing, taking back a Note and Deed of Trust. Then he went to the Bank and borrowed money and secured it with his Deed of Trust.

Now, he is probably using the Note payments to make the payments on the loan he has just signed at the Bank.

He already has his money, the cash from the loan. But he also has a loan that he is responsible for, and he has a Note that could go bad. He would probably like to get out of the situation.

And you can help him do that, and probably put some more money in his pocket.

Here's why.

Say the Seller Financing Note was for $100,000. When he got a loan against it, the Bank probably loaned him $60,000. You can buy his Note for $70,000 and he can pay off his $60,000 loan and keep the $10,000 to go with the $60,000 that he already has from the Bank.

He has $70,000 cash and no debt.

To determine your ROI on this deal, see "How To Analyze The Deal" below.

HOW TO EVALUATE NOTES

There are two steps for evaluating a Note.

The first step is to look at the ratio between the Fair Market Value (FMV) of the property that is securing the Note, and the Principal Balance remaining on the Note.

And the second step is to determine the risk factor related to the payments on the Note, or the credit worthiness of the Borrower.

First, let's look at the value of the property.

Assume that the Fair Market Value (FMV) of the property was $100,000 at the time that the financing was done and the Note was created.

The Buyer probably paid down $30,000.

The Note will probably be for $70,000.

Since the date the Note was created, the FMV of the property has probably gone up, say 6% per year.

At the same time, the Principal Balance of the Note has gone down because each payment is a combination of interest, and principal reduction. It has not gone down by very much, but it has gone down some. To determine how much the Principal has been reduced, you can do an Amortization Schedule by going to the website that I identified above, and just entering the Loan Amount, Interest Rate, Term, and Payment Amount. You only have to enter three of the four, and the Calculator will figure the other one. It will also show you all of the payments, the amount of interest and principal making up each one, and the Principal Balance remaining after each payment.

These are the projected numbers on paper.

And they are very helpful.

But to get real numbers regarding the FMV of the property, you can do two things.

The first thing is to go to the office of the agency that handles the assessment and collection of property taxes in your area, usually called something like the Tax Appraisal District, and look at the records for the property. These are "public records" and should be open to you. You will see the Assessed Value of the property for purposes of assessing the property taxes. These numbers are not completely reliable, but they are pretty close. A local Realtor can tell you the percentage by which they are usually off.

The second thing that you can do is pay a Real Estate Professional to provide you with what is called a BPO – a Brokers Price Opinion. It does not have to be by a Broker, it can be done by anyone knowledgeable about local real estate. It will cost a few hundred dollars, and it will be about as close to the actual FMV as you can get.

Now that you know the FMV of the property, and the Principal Balance of the loan, it is time to look at the party responsible for paying the Note, called the Obligor, but whom we will call the Borrower.

The best way to assess your risk of default on the Note is to get a Credit Report on the Borrower. There are laws concerning this process and you will probably need the Borrower's permission to obtain a report. If you explain to the Borrower who you are and why you want a Credit Report, and offer to give them a free copy of it, they might agree. But you should be careful here, and always respect the rights of the individual, just as you would want your own rights to be respected.

For me, one of my basic rules in business is that the best predictor of future behavior of an individual is the past behavior of that individual. It almost always holds true.

So, you want to know if the Borrower has made all of the payments on time since the inception of the Note.

First, you ask the Note holder for this information. He will probably tell you that all payments have been made on time. But there is a way that you can verify this.

In fact, there are two ways.

The holder of the Note is receiving interest income with each payment and will be required to report this interest income at the end of the tax year on Schedule B of his Form 1040, and identify the source of the interest income as something like "John Smith Note" and the amount of interest received. You can ask him for a copy of each Schedule B for the years the Note has been in existence, and compare the amounts reported to the Amortization Schedule.

The other way to verify the payments is to ask the Note holder for a copy of the Form 1099 that he is required to send to the Borrower showing the amount of "mortgage interest" paid on the Note during the tax year. You can also check this figure against the Amortization Schedule.

These two techniques won't tell you if the payments were made on time, but they will tell you if all of the payments were made.

HOW TO ANALYZE THE DEAL

I love numbers.

And even if you don't, you should at least like these.

There is a Real Estate Lien Note in the original Principal Amount of $100,000 and Interest Rate of 7%, with Payments of $1,980.12 for five years, or 60 months.

The Note is one year old and has a Remaining Principal Balance of $82,690.22.

You purchase the Note for $70,000 cash.

Did you just make $12,690.22 in Profit, which is 18.13%?

Well, No, not unless you received no money for eleven months and then at the end of the twelfth month you received $82,690.22. That would be a $12,690.22 Profit in a one-year period, and would represent an 18.13% return on your investment.

But, Notes are different.

The return on your investment, your ROI, is received in a fixed number of equal monthly payments.

The ROI for the Lender in the original Note was 7%.

In order to determine what your ROI will be now that you own the Note, you must use the Calculation that creates the Amortization Schedule.

The original Note holder invested $100,000 for 60 months and received payments of $1,980.12. His ROI was 7%.

You have invested $70,000 and will receive 48 remaining monthly payments of $1,980.22. What is your ROI?

If you plug your numbers into the Amortization Schedule Calculator, and hit the Interest calculator button, you will see that your ROI is 15.89%.

You can analyze any deal this same way, even using it to calculate the offer you will make for the note.

For example, assume that in the instance above, you want to make 18.0% on your investment. You just plug in 18%, 48 payments, and $1,980.22 and hit the Loan Amount button, and it will tell you that you should pay $67,411.76 for the Note.

HOW TO PURCHASE NOTES

When you purchase a Real Estate Lien Note, you will need two legal documents to effect the transfer.

One is an Assignment of Real Estate Lien Note, and the other is a Transfer of Lien.

These will be called by different names in States that use the Mortgage instead of the Deed of Trust to create the lien on the property.

You will need an Attorney to prepare these documents, and you can either Close the transaction in his office, or you can have it done at a Title Company.

You will also need the Attorney to draft a Purchase Agreement between you and the current Note holder outlining the terms of your agreement. If you require the Note holder to take the Note back if it goes into Default within a certain period of time, you need this agreement in writing. There are other terms that should go into the agreement and you should discuss these with the Attorney.

Also, when the original Note was created, the current Note holder received a Mortgagee's Title Policy or a Lender's Title Policy issued by the Title Company after searching title, which will reimburse the Lender for any loss caused by a defect in title.

You should require the current Note Holder to provide you with an Endorsement to that Policy if such is available, or require that the search be brought current by the Title Company, showing new liens or defects in the meantime.

And you should also have the existing Liability Insurance Policy amended, or get an Endorsement, changing the Loss Payee from the current Note holder to you.

This is not a comprehensive list, and you will know what else you need as you proceed with the deal.

CONCLUSION

Note Investing is probably the simplest and cleanest of all of the Ten Other Real Estate Investments.

Once you find the Note and evaluate it, you decide how much you want to make on your investment, and make your offer.

In the beginning, things will be slow, and you will be investing a lot of time establishing your presence in the Real Estate Investing community.

But after a year or two, word of mouth will be generating enough calls that you will have all of the deals that you want to look at.

You need to have the funds to operate, obviously, and you need to either have the required knowledge, or have a plan to acquire the knowledge fairly quickly, and then you need to operate like a professional.

This business can fit any ambition of any Real Estate Investor.

You can remain an individual with a portfolio of Notes that return a nice monthly income, and occasionally are paid off, and provide funds to purchase another Note.

Or you can create an LLC with shares sold to investors, and the pool of funds used to find and purchase Notes that provide income to the investors as well as yourself.

Many people turn to this type of investing after retiring from another business or profession with their retirement funds. It allows them to stay active, and also to earn upwards of 15% on their money, while being in complete control of their finances instead of turning their money over to someone else.

CHAPTER 4

WHOLESALING

OVERVIEW

The activity that is known today as "Wholesaling" has existed for a long time, far longer than the current use of the term "Wholesaling" has existed, and the activity does not actually involve "wholesaling" anything.

If you are thinking about getting involved with Wholesaling, you need to understand what it is, and understand what it is not.

First, we'll do what it is not.

It is not "selling your interest in the property," "selling the contract," or "selling the property."

You don't own the property, an interest in the property, or the contract.

Now, let's talk about what "Wholesaling" is.

This is not rocket science.

If you sign a Contract with the owner of real estate to purchase that real estate under certain terms and conditions, you are a party to a Contract.

As a party to the Contract, you can assign your interest in that Contract to another person, if the Contract terms do not prohibit the assignment, and then the other person to whom you assign the Contract, called the Assignee, can complete the Contract.

It's as simple as that.

In order to decide if this type of investing is right for you, you need to know what is actually involved. So we will use the elements of a regular real estate investment for comparison.

We will look at:

1.) Income.

2.) Expenses.

3.) Cash Flow.

4.) Appreciation.

5.) Leverage.

6.) Tax Advantages.

INCOME

The income from Wholesaling real estate is a one-time event.

It happens when you sign a document called an Assignment of Contract, or Assignment of Interest in a Contract, or complete the Assignment paragraph in the Contract itself, if the Contract contains such a section.

If you sign a Contract to purchase a house for $40,000 and you find someone willing to pay $45,000 to own that house because he can do a certain amount of rehab, making the house worth much more, then he is willing to pay you $5,000 to assign that Contract to him so that he can purchase the house instead of you.

You might be paid the $5,000 at the time you assign the Contract, but the Assignee is assuming the risk of the deal falling apart before it closes. So, the Assignment will probably provide that you will be paid $5,000 at Closing from the funds that the Assignee/Buyer will bring to the Closing for payment of his expenses.

And you will not be required to be present at the Closing. Your check will be cut, just like the Surveyor's check, for instance, and you can pick it up later.

Your total income will be a one-time payment that you receive in return for assigning the Contract to the new Buyer.

EXPENSES

In Wholesaling, your expenses will be whatever money you spend in trying to find the property and get it under Contract.

This might be sending out postcards, running ads in newspapers or trade sheets, printing and putting up signs, and so forth.

As far as the actual property conveyance is concerned, you will have no expenses, because you are not involved in the transaction. You have assigned the Contract and are no longer a party.

Whether you have any Earnest Money in the deal is another matter, and I cover that in the next section called "Buying."

CASH FLOW

Unlike other Real Estate Investing, there is no cash flow with Wholesaling.

It's a one-time deal.

You assign the Contract, and you receive a one-time payment.

APPRECIATION

Again, unlike other Real Estate Investing, you are not taking title to anything, so there is no asset which might appreciate in value while you own it.

LEVERAGE

Leverage is one of the four pillars of Real Estate Investing, but in the case of Wholesaling, it doesn't apply.

You have not borrowed any money, or bought any property, or paid any interest or principal.

TAX ADVANTAGES

You will have no tax advantages in Wholesaling, because you never become the owner of rental real estate.

The tax laws are very favorable to real estate

investors, but Wholesalers are just conducting a business, never owning any real estate, and the income is ordinary business income, and will be taxable as such.

BUSINESS ENTITY

Read about business entities in Chapter 1 – Hard Money Lending. The same information applies here.

BUYING

The key to the Wholesaling business is "the buy."

In fact, "the buy" is almost the entire business, since the only thing you will be doing after getting the property under contract is to sign an Assignment of Contract.

The Contract is really your entire business.

If you screw up the Contract, the deal can fall apart at any time, and you might not be able to just walk away from it.

If you don't have a strong, air-tight Contract, you will also have trouble finding an Assignee willing to even give you the time of day, much less pay you a large fee to step into your shoes as the party to the Contract.

The Contract is all you have, since you don't really intend to buy the property.

Therefore, you need to have the best Contract you could possibly have.

So, OK, what should you be doing?

Well, let's look at:

1.) The Contract.

2.) Earnest Money.

3.) Inspection Period.

THE CONTRACT

Most of the activity surrounding the buying and selling of real estate involves Realtors.

The Realtors are members of the National Association of Realtors, referred to as NAR.

These Realtors are also member of the same type of Association for the State in which they are licensed as Realtors. For instance, in Texas, the Realtors are members of NAR, and are also members of the Texas Association of Realtors, known as TAR.

But Realtors are licensed by the State, not by their Association.

The agency of the State that licenses and regulates Realtors is usually called something like the (State) Real Estate Commission.

For instance, in Texas the group is called the Texas Real Estate Commission, and is referred to as TREC.

TREC creates forms for use in the business of real estate and it mandates that Realtors use the forms when they handle a sale.

These are available to the public, and you should use them to learn what is in a Contract.

To find the agency in your State, go to:

www.arello.org/index.cfm/resourses/regulatory-agencies/#region1.

As I said before, you are in the Contract business. The Contract is your only asset. You should learn everything that you can about it.

COMPLETING THE CONTRACT

Although, as a Wholesaler, you are operating in the business of Real Estate Investing, your product is not actually real estate.

You don't need a system for buying, managing, and selling real estate.

Your product is Contracts.

Therefore, you need to have a management system for your products.

As a Wholesaler, it will probably be necessary for you to have about 40 offers out there for every one that will work out for you.

But if you try to handle 40 written contracts by hand, you won't have any time to find the deals that you need to stay in business.

You need a system that will manage those 40 Contract offers for you electronically, and that will allow you to access them on any device from any location.

The answer is a cloud-based content management system (CMS) called PDFfiller.

You can find it at www.pdffiller.com.

It costs $6.00 per month for the Personal version, and you can try it first for 30 days free.

It is not only a PDF editor, but it has a library of 25 million fillable documents, many of them with Instructions.

The library includes the Purchase Agreements from the State agencies that I discussed above, and will have the specific ones that you need for your State. You can even create your own documents and forms and store them in your library.

You can access a form, fill it out, eSign it, send it out for signature, and then be notified when it has been signed.

You can store all of your forms, and manage them from anywhere.

Your data is secured with bank-level encryption.

Everything you need to know about PDFfiller is in this review:

Https://reviews.financeonline.com/p/pdfiller.

If you have a more efficient system, then you should use it.

But I like this one a lot, and I do almost everything else with paper.

EARNEST MONEY

This is the part of Wholesaling that causes me to cringe.

And you should also be bothered by it.

There are books and articles that tell you that you do not need money to Wholesale real estate, that you just sign a Purchase Agreement, then find someone else to give you money in return for an Assignment.

There are other people like you out there trying to Wholesale who have no money and think that they don't need any. Then they try to do a deal, and learn the truth.

Some even manage to get the Purchase Agreement signed without putting up Earnest Money.

Let's talk about that.

A Purchase Agreement is a Contract.

A Contract is a legal instrument, and as such, it has a description in the body of law that states what the elements of a valid Contract are. If these elements are not present, it is not a Contract.

The legal elements of a Contract are:

1.) Offer,

2.) Acceptance, and

3.) Consideration.

It has always been so.

In a Purchase Agreement:

1.) The Offer is by the Seller of the Property offering to sell you 123 Main for $50,000.

2.) The Acceptance is you signing the Purchase Agreement agreeing to buy 123 Main for $50,000.

3.) Upon the signing of the Purchase Agreement, the Consideration from the Seller is his commitment that he will not sell the Property to anyone else for the duration of the term of the Agreement, and the Consideration from you is the Earnest Money that you deposit. What?

The Real Estate Gurus didn't tell you about the $10,000 that you need to do this, did they?

Or even $5,000. Or $2,000.

It doesn't matter, because you don't have any money. That's why you're doing Wholesaling instead of Flipping or Buy and Hold. You were told you didn't need any money.

Well, you do.

THE INSPECTION PERIOD

The Purchase Agreement is a legal Contract, and, like all Contracts, should be entered into in good faith. This is a concept of law, a legal requirement.

The Wholesaler is in breach of this requirement the minute he signs the Purchase Agreement, because it probably says, "Seller agrees to sell and convey to Buyer and Buyer agrees to buy from Seller the property defined below."

The Wholesaler (Buyer) has no intention of buying the property.

The Wholesaler's intention is to prevent the Seller from selling his property to anyone else while the Wholesaler finds another Buyer who would be willing to pay the Seller $5,000 to $10,000 more than the Contract price, and then the Wholesaler will assign the Contract to the second Buyer in return for receiving a $5,000 to $10,000 fee himself.

To further mislead the Seller, the Wholesaler will ask for terms in the Purchase Contract providing for an "Inspection Period" to give him time to peddle the Contract, and if he can't find a Buyer, to cancel the Contract.

In the world of real estate, an Inspection Period is the time during which a Buyer has the opportunity to perform Due Diligence on the property he intends to buy.

This time period must be agreed upon by both parties to the Contract, Buyer and Seller, at the beginning when the Contract is signed.

If there is an Inspection Period, it can range from one day to 30 days, or more.

But in our discussion the Wholesaler has no intention of inspecting the property because he doesn't care what condition it is in, because he isn't going to buy it.

If the Wholesaler can find a Buyer, he assigns the Contract, and the new Buyer takes over, and either buys the property or forfeits the Earnest Money Deposit.

If the Wholesaler does not find a Buyer, the Wholesaler will do whatever the terms of the Contract require him to do to notify the Seller that he is canceling the Contract.

If the Seller agrees, both parties will sign a document canceling the Contract and instructing the holder of the Earnest Money, usually the Title Company, to release it to the Buyer.

The Title Company that is holding the Earnest Money Deposit is acting as a Fiduciary in this situation, because it is holding money belonging to someone else as an escrow agent, which is the legal definition.

However, if the Seller feels like he was misled and refuses to sign the Release, the Title Company will hold onto the Earnest Money, and say, "The facts are in dispute, and I require a Court Order instructing me how to disburse the funds."

The Wholesaler, if he's smart, does not want to go to Court, and will probably just lose his Earnest Money Deposit.

So be careful. The inspection period is not the silver bullet that will get you out of the Contract.

MANAGING YOUR BUSINESS

Deciding to become a Wholesaler involves answering the following questions.

1.) Do I have the time required?

2.) Do I have the skills required?

If you don't have the time or ability, nothing else matters.

But if you do have the time, and you think you either have, or can learn, the ability to do it correctly, then you might have a Business Model just waiting for you.

And it is just that – a business.

TIME REQUIRED

You can probably do this part-time, as an individual, working around a full-time job. There is a lot of waiting involved, and you can use that to your advantage.

But doing it part-time will limit your success and your growth as a business.

If you start doing it part-time, and enjoy some success, you will probably switch to full-time after a few months, because if you can do it successfully, this is one of the most profitable ways to make a living.

I don't have a plan for you. There isn't space here to lay out the entire procedure for you to get started, and what you will have to do.

But you can learn it.

You just have to read the material that is available and find what works for you.

But as I have cautioned before, you should be suspicious of everything you read.

So, be careful.

There is no single model for everyone.

SKILLS REQUIRED

This is what makes the business of Wholesaling a real mystery to me.

People think they should do Wholesaling because they are Newbies and don't yet know anything about Real Estate Investing, and this is the simplest form of investing.

It is not.

Think about it. When you decide to make an offer, you need to know what your buyer will pay you to assign the Contract. And that's where the complications come in.

Do you know what the ultimate market value of this property will be? Of course not, you're totally inexperienced in this business.

Do you know whether it is ready to market or if it will need repairs, and which items need attention, and how much it will cost to do the repairs, and which repairs will add the most value? Of course not, same reason.

Do you know how much a Hard Money Lender will agree to loan on this property?

Well, you get the idea.

Wholesaling is not a simple business. It is very complicated.

You are doing the same thing as the investor who is Flipping and the investor who is doing Buy and Hold. You are just doing the first step in the whole process that they go through, and then turning it over to them. But the decisions in the first step all depend on the facts concerning all of the later steps, and you don't understand these.

Look at the Chapters on Hard Money Lending and Flipping to see what the entire process looks like, and decide if you have the knowledge do this first step.

You are the only one who knows if you have the skills required to be successful.

LIABILITY

In the world of Real Estate Investing, the term "liability" usually refers to two things.

The first is the liability for the debt on the property. This is a business liability.

The second is personal liability for anything that might happen on the property that leads to a lawsuit, and possibly a judgment. This is personal liability.

You will have neither of these, because you will not own the property.

But there is a very real liability that you must be concerned with.

I have heard a lot of conversations and read a lot of content where the Wholesaler is depicted as without any worries in the world, because he has a "walk-away" contract.

Look at the Section above called "The Contract" to refresh your understanding of what a Contract is.

If you enter into a Contract, you are taking on obligations and responsibilities that you will be expected to stand behind. This is serious business. If that Contract didn't really mean anything, as you are being told, then why do Contracts exist?

Do you think that Contracts were created so that someone could tie up another person's property and then either make $5,000 assigning the Contract, or just walk away?

Contracts were created to memorialize the understanding of both parties, and to manage the rights and responsibilities of both parties to a transaction.

Most business lawsuits that I have seen in the past 35 years involve allegations of Breach of Contract, and many of them also include a claim of Fraud.

Be very careful with how you conduct yourself.

TAXATION

Your income as a Wholesaler is not income derived from real estate investing.

As such, it is not passive income.

It is ordinary business income and it will be taxed at your personal income tax rate.

In addition, it is also Self-Employment income, and will be subject to an additional 15.3% SE tax.

SELLING

"Selling," in the case of Wholesalers, means "assigning" in return for a payment.

But it is still not selling, because, as explained earlier, you cannot sell an incomplete, contingency, Contract.

The only time that you might "sell" is when you do a "double-closing."

And a double-closing is not Wholesaling.

A double-closing is when you complete the purchase of the real estate under the Purchase Agreement that you entered into, instead of assigning the Contract to another entity. And then, after that Closing, you immediately sell the real estate to another party, in another Closing.

The two events are completely separate and unrelated, except that both involve the same real estate.

A double-closing is probably a Flip, if it is anything. But it is not Wholesaling.

CONCLUSION

I have handled thousands of real estate closings as an Attorney and as the owner of a Title Company, and many of those closings involved Sales Contracts that had been assigned to a subsequent purchaser.

I am totally familiar with both the law and the process.

And yet, I read top-selling books today that contain total nonsense, and sound like they were just made up at the time they were written.

More likely, they are embellished versions of the canned programs that are being sold by the Real Estate Gurus. The author bought one and wrote a book.

Be very careful with this Wholesaling process.

It is very deceptive at its core.

You are signing a legal document that the Seller believes signifies your intention to buy his property, and that is not true.

You intend to sell his property, not buy it.

And if you can't sell it, you intend to walk away and abandon him.

Don't be lulled into a sense of comfort by those who try to convince you that this is completely legal, moral, ethical, and honest.

That's your decision, and it is one you will carry with you forever.

CHAPTER 5

FLIPPING

OVERVIEW

Only two of the Ten Other Real Estate Investments in this book involve actually owning real estate, and this is one of them, although this one has no tenants.

"Flipping Properties" is the Real Estate Investing business that sets itself apart from the others.

Flipping is the practice of buying real estate, rehabilitating it, and then selling it for profit.

It is a short-term activity, and distinctly different from the form of investing known as "Buy and Hold," which involves buying real estate, possibly rehabilitating it, and then renting or leasing it to tenants over a number of years in return for rental income, with the added bonus of property value appreciation.

Flipping does not have the most important benefit of Buy And Hold rental real estate.

Investing in rental real estate is considered a passive activity, with passive income and losses, unless you are a Real Estate Professional.

But, if you are flipping properties you will probably be considered by the IRS to be a real estate "dealer."

Even if some of the properties are held in your name for more than 12 months before they are sold, you still cannot claim Long Term Capital Gains status on the income.

The properties will still be considered "inventory for sale" if the dominant characteristic of your business activities is "buying and selling real estate."

You are a dealer.

You are operating a business, just like a furniture store.

Your income will be taxable as ordinary business income, and this could significantly increase your tax liability, because ordinary income is also subject to the 15.3% Self-Employment Tax.

But let's analyze Flipping the same way that we would look at any form of Real Estate Investing, and discuss each element.

1.) Income.

2.) Expenses.

3.) Cash Flow.

4.) Appreciation.

5.) Leverage.

6.) Tax Advantages.

INCOME

Income from Flipping will occur when you sell the property that you have bought and rehabbed.

It will be your profit, the difference between what you received for the property, and what you paid for it plus all of the costs of rehabbing and selling.

For Example, you paid a Wholesaler $5,000 to assign his Purchase Agreement to you, and then you bought the property for $40,000 and spent $20,000 rehabbing the property.

That's $65,000.

You sold the property for $100,000.

That leaves $35,000.

Your transaction costs for the purchase was $2,000 and your transaction cost for the sale was $3,000.

That leaves $30,000 profit.

This does not take into account the expenses of operating your business, or the costs of funds if you borrowed money to buy the property and do the work. See Chapter 1 on Hard Money Lending for information on this.

This is only the income on this one project.

EXPENSES

The key to Flipping is being able to correctly estimate the cost of rehabbing the property.

The easier decision is what to pay for the property, and that depends on the After Repair Value (ARV), which I cover below.

Estimating rehab costs will involve inspecting the property, and knowing from your experience what will have to be done in order to sell the property when it is put on the market.

This will consist of materials costs and labor costs.

The expenses we are dealing with here are just the expenses of the project.

The expenses of running your business are a separate category of expenses.

CASH FLOW

There is no cash flow in Flipping, because it is a one-time sale, once the property has been purchased and rehabbed.

APPRECIATION

Appreciation, in the general sense, means the normal and natural increase in the value of the property over the passage of time.

In that regard, there is no appreciation involved in Flipping.

But there is definitely an appreciation factor, and it is the "forced appreciation" that is the result of rehabbing the property.

The plan is that if a distressed property is worth $40,000 on the open market, it can be purchased and another $20,000 spent on rehabilitation, and the resulting property will be worth much more than the sum of the two amounts.

It is no longer a distressed property, it is an attractive and very livable property that will attract a lot of buyers.

The appreciation in value comes from changing the character of the property.

LEVERAGE

Leverage usually means, in Real Estate Investing, the use of a small amount of your own money, combined with borrowed funds, to hold a property over time and receive all of the benefit of the property's increase in value, even though all of the money invested was not from your own funds.

Since Flipping does not involve the holding of property over a sufficient amount of time to generate market appreciation, leverage does not really apply.

There is, however, another type of leverage that is involved.

The Flipper will probably borrow the funds to buy the property.

If he does, it will probably be $30,000 of the $40,000 purchase price, plus all of the $20,000 needed to rehab the property, for a total of $50,000.

He will probably pay 10% plus two points for the six-month period that he will be rehabbing the property. This will be a cost of $6,000 for the Hard Money Loan.

So his total investment will be the $10,000 that the Hard Money Lender required him to put up as a Down Payment on the property.

If he sells the property for the $100,000 that is the estimated After Repair Value (ARV), that's pretty good leverage on a deal.

He used $10,000 of his own money, borrowed the rest, and ended up with $44,000.

What he borrowed was his leverage.

TAX ADVANTAGES

There are actually no tax advantages for the Flipper, at least as that term is used in the rest of Real Estate Investing.

But in fact, there is probably a tax disadvantage, because his income will be considered ordinary income, taxable at his personal income tax rate, plus another 15.3% Self-Employment Tax.

This is assuming that he will be operating as an LLC with the status of Disregarded Entity.

He could also consider an LLC with S Corp status, but the benefit would probably be very small.

See Chapter 1 on Hard Money Lending for a complete discussion of business entities, specifically the LLC.

BUSINESS ENTITY

Read about business entities in Chapter 1 – Hard Money Lending. The same information applies here.

BUYING

The Flipper will probably do his own searching for the properties that he will buy to rehab. He might also buy from a Wholesaler who has already found the property and gotten it under contract. He might even have prior arrangements with individuals who know exactly what he is looking for, sometimes referred to as "bird dogs."

The Flipper will bind the contract with an Earnest Money Deposit, and he will make sure that the Purchase Agreement provides for a reasonable amount of time to inspect the property to make sure that he can even do what he plans to do.

If he knows how to do so, he will check the county tax records to make sure that there are no delinquent taxes.

And if he knows how, he will do a preliminary check of the county real estate records to see if there are any liens or pending litigation regarding the property.

Then he will take the contract to the Title Company, and he will also order a Survey if the property is not in a platted subdivision, and maybe even if it is.

If he has his own money, he will use it.

If he has a guaranteed source of funds, he will tap it.

If he operates from project to project, he will talk to his Hard Money Lender.

The Closing on the purchase of the property will go just like any other Closing. It is just a buyer purchasing real estate. If there is a Hard Money Lender involved, there might be some specific differences. See Chapter 1.

SELLING

Showtime. The Flipper will probably want to save the $6,000 real estate commission, and so will probably not list the property with a Realtor.

And there really is no need to do so.

Just putting a sign in front of the property during the six months that the rehab is going on, will get about a hundred times the attention that will come from just listing the property.

Do a cleanup, and hold an Open House.

It's not easy to do, but if you're only doing it twice a year, you should be able to handle it.

MANAGING YOUR BUSINESS

Managing a Flipping business is like managing a Construction Company, except that you don't have to put up with the property owner, because that's you.

You will need to know how to do the work, and you will need to know how to buy the right materials.

You need to be able to do this yourself.

It's possible to hire other people to do this while you are working at your other full-time job, but it's a very tough way to go.

This is a business that cranks up early in the morning and goes until there is a natural break in the activities. You really need to be there, especially if there are problems cropping up, and there are always problems.

In addition to anything else you are doing, you are basically the Business Manager.

You need to know how to do that, or know a lot and learn the rest very quickly.

TIME REQUIRED

Your time required will be different for each part of the project, because you will be doing different things and they will each require different periods of time.

In the beginning, you will be gathering information, putting together your plan, and you will just spend a solid eight hours a day, maybe more.

There will be times when you are waiting for something like the Survey, or the Closing, and you will almost have down time.

But once you get everyone scheduled for the jobs, you might work some 12-hour days, because, for example, if the painter is coming tomorrow, you need to be finished with what you are doing today and have everybody out of the house. You can't reschedule painters and roofers.

As I said, you will need to be a Business Manager, and that's a much bigger job than most people realize.

SKILLS REQUIRED

You pretty much have to know how to do everything.

Not that you need to know how to do the plumbing, but you need to know enough about it to know what needs to be done, and whether it is being done correctly.

The same for electrical, painting, tile, the HVAC system, etc.

The more of the skilled labor you can do yourself, the less your expenses will be, and the higher your profit.

The best skill that you can learn is carpentry, because that will be required from start to finish.

At some point, you will have a favorite list of "subs," the sub-contractors that will bid on the cabinet work, the flooring, the plumbing, and anything else that you need.

MONEY REQUIRED

The money required will be the purchase price of the property, and the cost of doing the rehab.

If the Flipper does not have the funds for either or both of these expenses, there are Hard Money Lenders who specialize is loaning funds for exactly this type of project. They will have a system in place, and the process will go very smoothly. The money will be available before the Title Company can get to the Closing.

So, if the Flipper has found a suitable property, and if he is qualified to do the project, the money required will usually be available.

LIABILITY

The liability involved in the project will be the usual liability for a construction job site.

The Flipper will have insurance to cover the possibility, and will also be operating as an LLC which will limit the personal liability that might arise from the activities of the business.

The liability involved with the loan, if one is used, involves not being able to repay it.

If this happens, the Lender is often happy to just receive the property in complete satisfaction, and release the Flipper from any responsibility.

TAXATION

The income is ordinary income, and will be taxable to the Flipper at his personal tax rate, and an additional 15.3% Self-Employment Tax.

CONCLUSION

Flipping is probably the most familiar of the Ten Other Real Estate Investments because it has been all over the TV screens for many years.

Just remember, those shows are entertainment, like the movies. They are not documentaries.

A lot of the information is correct, but a lot of it is not.

And about 90% of what you need to know to run a successful Flipping business will not be learned from watching the shows.

Flipping is a business. The primary tool of any business is Business Management. You will not be successful without learning it. And yes, there is an App for that. It is used by people who don't know how to manage a business.

The other requirement for success is some level of construction knowledge and skill.

You can start without it and learn it, but you cannot just turn it over to someone else.

You will need to put the project together yourself, and you will need to be on the job every day to make sure everything is done correctly.

And then you will have to sell the property.

Fortunately, there are no Apps for those. You either learn them or you go out of business before you have lost too much money.

Flipping is where the real professionals are operating in the world of Real Estate Investing. They make the most money, and they eventually move up into more complicated and more profitable activities.

The knowledge and skills of Flipping is the best foundation you can have for your entire career in Real Estate Investing.

CHAPTER 6

SECTION 121 INVESTING

OVERVIEW

Would you would like to own 20 high-quality income properties in 40 years, completely tax-free, and without competing with all of the other Real Estate Investors?

How about 15 in 30 years? Or 10 in 20 years?

And you can do it without even actually buying a rental property!

Then this Chapter is for you.

Here's how that would work.

What you buy is a personal residence of your choice, one that meets all of the needs and comforts of you and your family.

This is probably something that you should be doing anyway.

Easy.

Then, every two years, you convert your personal residence into a rental property, after having had two years to find the perfect tenant.

And then you buy another personal residence, after having had two years to shop for the right one.

But there's more to the plan than that.

After owning the property as a personal residence for two years, and as a rental property for three years, you can sell it, and pay zero taxes on the five years of Capital Gains that accrued while you owned it, with no requirement to reinvest the money.

Your only cost will be the Depreciation Recapture for the three years that it was rental property, and you're probably just giving back money you have already saved by claiming the Depreciation Allowance on your personal tax return.

And it gets still better.

If you want to keep the rental property, and add it to your investment portfolio, you can buy the property yourself, from yourself, using an S-Corp, and still not pay any Capital Gains taxes.

This is all possible because of the best Section in the Internal Revenue Code: Section 121.

BUSINESS ENTITY

Read about business entities in Chapter 1 – Hard Money Lending. The same information applies here.

SECTION 121

Of all the assets that you own, there is only one that you can sell without having to pay taxes on your profit.

Internal Revenue Code Section 121 covers the sale of a primary residence owned and occupied by the taxpayer.

To qualify for using Section 121, a taxpayer must own the property and live in the property for at least two years out of the five years prior to the sale.

A single taxpayer can exclude $250,000 of Capital Gains from such a sale.

A married taxpayer can exclude $500,000 of Capital Gain.

The husband and wife must have both lived in the house for the qualifying years, and they must file a joint tax return. The house can be in the name of either of them or in the names of both.

This does not mean that you must own the house for five years. It means that you have a five-year period in which to accumulate the two qualifying years of ownership and occupancy.

The qualifying years do not have to be consecutive or continuous. You can satisfy the requirement in smaller increments.

You can use Section 121 to exempt your Capital Gains taxes on the sale of a primary residence every two years.

The rules for Section 121 are fairly simple, and you can find more information in the IRS Publication 523, "Selling Your Home," and in IRS Publication 527, "Residential Rental Property," both available at www.irs. gov.

INVESTING PLAN

The main feature of the Section 121 Investing plan is the flexibility.

You can just utilize Section 121 and buy, convert, and sell.

Or you can combine Section 121 with a lifetime plan of Real Estate Investing and build a portfolio of quality investment properties without all of the usual hassles involved in Real Estate Investing, and without ever paying any Capital Gains taxes.

BUY, CONVERT AND SELL

If you just want to spend two years finding the perfect tenant, and then convert your personal residence to a rental property, you can do that.

And after another three years, you can sell the property, and pay no Capital Gains taxes on the sale.

Now understand, a $250,000 residence will probably be worth $345,750 after five years, assuming the historic 6.7% annual asset appreciation for real estate.

That amounts to $95,750 in Capital Gains.

If you are in the 15% CG tax bracket, you will save $14,363 in taxes.

If you are in the 20% CG tax bracket, you will save $19,150 in taxes.

Of course, you will pay up to 25% tax on the recapture of the depreciation claimed for the three years that the property was being used as a rental property.

That is called Depreciation Recapture, and the amount here would be $6,818. This is about the same amount of taxes that you would have saved in the three years by claiming the Depreciation on your tax return.

If you choose to go this route, here's what your investing plan with look like.

Beginning in the fifth year, you will have three properties.

The first property is House #1 that you bought at the beginning of the first year, and converted to rental property at the beginning of the third year, when you bought House #2.

The second property is House #2 that you bought at the beginning of the third year, and converted to rental property at the beginning of the fifth year, when you bought House #3.

The third property is House #3 that you just bought.

At the end of this year, the fifth year, and before the beginning of the sixth year, you will sell House #1 and avoid all Capital Gains taxes under the provisions of Section 121.

Every two years thereafter you will buy a new residence, and convert your existing residence to a rental property.

Every two years you will sell the oldest rental property before the fifth year of ownership to take advantage of Section 121.

At any one time during your plan, either you will own one residence and one rental property, or one residence and two rental properties.

Now, let's look at what you will be getting.

Let's use the $95,750 in asset appreciation for each of the properties over the five-year period. That amounts to $19,150 each year.

That means that during the years when you own two properties, you will make $38,300 in asset appreciation that year, and in the years when you own three properties, you will enjoy $57,450 in asset appreciation, for the single year.

This does not take into account the fact that the properties will probably rent for 1% of their value, or about $3,000 per month. About half of this should be profit to you, but let's be conservative and say $1,250 instead of $1,500.

That means that your annual cash flow from rents should be about $15,000 in the years when you have one rental property, and $30,000 in the years when you have two rental properties.

Together, with cash flow and asset appreciation, your yearly benefits should alternate between $53,300 and $87,450.

That's not bad for owning one or two rental properties that you created by just converting your residence every two years.

And an important side effect of all this is that after you sell the first few rental properties, you will probably be able to start paying cash for each new residence.

But as good as this is, even better things happen when you combine Section 121 with lifetime Real Estate Investing, and sell the properties to yourself.

SELL TO YOURSELF

You don't really sell to yourself, but "same as."

You select this option if you want to continue to own the rental property, even though you are selling it, at the end of the five years, and still eliminate the Capital Gains taxes.

To do so, you must have what the IRS considers "a qualified sale."

That's why you can't just sell the property to yourself, or form an LLC and sell the property to the LLC.

You must sell to a separate legal entity, and that must be either a C Corp or an S Corp, and the better of the two will be the S Corp.

Now, again, this is not an LLC that files Form 8832 Entity Classification Election and chooses to be taxed as an S Corp. This is a real S Corp, which means that it is a C Corp that has filed Form 2553 electing to be treated as an S Corp.

The S Corp will be a new business entity, and the traditional lending environment might not be a friendly one, even if you are willing to do a personal Guaranty on the loan. In other words, Banks will offer you coffee and a smile in order to not piss you off, but they will probably not offer you a loan. You might have to go to a Private Lender.

If your finances are established already, and you do have a Bank who wants to keep your business, and you end up getting a loan, it will be a Commercial Loan instead of the Residential Loan you have on the property (even though the property has already been a commercial property for three years), so the term of the new loan will be shorter and the interest rate will be higher.

The Sales Price will have to be the Fair Market Value (FMV) of the property so that the transaction will "pass muster" under the rule that requires what is called "an arm's length transaction," which means that you sold it for what it would bring in the open market, with willing buyers and willing sellers.

Your Residential Loan is not assumable, and the sale will trigger the Due On Sale Clause in the Deed of Trust, so you must get a new loan, and the new loan will be for much more than the Remaining Principal Balance of the existing loan.

That's the bad news.

Here's the good news.

If we use the above example of the $250,000 personal residence, you will be receiving about $110,000 in net cash proceeds when you sell the property for about $345,000.

So, before the Closing, you can get a short-term loan for $110,000 and loan it to your S Corp, so that the

S Corp can use it as a Down Payment on the property, and then qualify for a 70% loan.

When you receive the $110,000 from the sale of the property, you pay back the short-term loan.

At this point, you will own an S Corp which owns a $345,000 investment property with a $235,000 mortgage and about $110,000 equity, and owes you $110,000.

As you can see, you just transferred your equity in the property to the S Corp, which you own, and which now has an increased Basis in the property for purposes of Depreciation and for purposes of computing future Capital Gains.

In four more years, the property will have appreciated to $447,000 and you can refinance and get the $110,000 out as a loan repayment, tax-free, of course, except for the interest.

Remember that Real Estate Investing is all about the future, and about creating future income with which you can plan your other activities.

But for now, you need to know about how to form an S Corp, and I refer you to my book "How To Choose Your Best Business Entity For Real Estate Investing" for exactly what to do, and how to do it.

BUILD YOUR PORTFOLIO

This is the section where we look at what will happen if you decide to use the plan of combining Section 121 and Real Estate Investing to build a real estate portfolio during your lifetime, instead of just using Section 121 to buy, convert and sell.

We need a scenario to create the numbers, so we will assume that you are 23 years old, either single or married, and beginning in 2020, you will buy and convert a $220,000 residence every two years, sell each property to your own S Corp at the end of the five-year Section 121 qualification period, and that you will retire at the age of 50.

At that point, you should have $8 Million in assets, and $40,000 monthly income.

1-2020 Buy #1

1-2022 Convert #1 to Rental, Buy #2

1-2024 Convert #2 to Rental, Buy #3

12-2024 Sell #1 to S Corp

1-2026 Convert #3 to Rental, Buy #4

12-2026 Sell #2 to S Corp

1-2028 Convert #4 to Rental, Buy #5

12-2028 Sell #3 to S Corp

1-2030 Convert #5 to Rental, Buy #6

12-2030 Sell #4 to S Corp

1-2032 Convert #6 to Rental, Buy #7

12-2032 Sell #5 to S Corp

1-2034 Convert #7 to Rental, Buy #8

12-2034 Sell #6 to S Corp

1-2036 Convert #8 to Rental, Buy #9

12-2036 Sell #7 to S Corp

1-2038 Convert #9 to Rental, Buy #10

12-2038 Sell #8 to S Corp

1-2040 Convert #10 to Rental, Buy #11

12-2040 Sell #9 to S Corp

1-2042 Convert #11 to Rental, Buy #12

12-2042 Sell #10 to S Corp

1-2044 Convert #12 to Rental, Buy #13

12-2044 Sell #11 to S Corp

1-2046 Convert #13 to Rental, Buy #14

12-2046 Sell #12 to S Corp

1-2047 Retire

Whew!

That looks like a lot of work, but it isn't.

Every two years, you converted a property to rental, bought a new residence, and sold a property to your S Corp.

In alternate years, you did nothing.

So, you are now 50 years old. Let's see what you have accomplished.

You are living in a residence that you just bought.

You have one rental property in your own name.

You own an S Corp that owns 12 quality rental properties.

What is the total FMV of all of the properties, assuming that they were bought for $220,000 and they have appreciated in value the historical average of 6.7% per year?

#1 = $1,187,674

#2 = $1,043,202

#3 = $916,304

#4 = $804,842

#5 = $706,939

#6 = $620,945

#7 = $545,411

#8 = $479,066

#9 = $420,791

#10 = $369,605

#11 = $324,645

#12 = $285,154

#13 = $250,467

#14 = $220,000

Total = $8,175,045

Assuming additionally that the debts on the properties were 15-year Commercial Loans when each of the properties was sold to the S Corp, seven of the loans are paid off, and the total balance remaining on the other seven is $975,176.

Your net worth in real estate is about $7.2 Million.

Now let's look at your monthly income.

Using the rule that a property will rent for an amount each month equal to 1% of the FMV, and the rule that your profit will be about half of the monthly rent, we come up with 1/2% of $8 Million.

That amount is $40,000 per month.

And that's where the analysis shows its faults.

We know that when each of these properties reaches the value of about $600,000 it would be sold, and three other $200,000 properties would be bought as Replacement Properties in a Section 1031 Exchange.

But the total numbers are correct.

The passage of time, the steady purchase of properties, and the annual appreciation of the properties will result in this level of wealth and early retirement.

If you have a plan that you can easily handle, and you stick to it, this will be you.

CONCLUSION

Section 121 Investing is about the most "part-time" type of Real Estate Investing that you can do, at least for the first few years.

And when the activity becomes more than part-time, or more than you want to do, along with a regular job, you can just hire a Property Management Company, and continue with your system by buying and selling every two years.

Even if you only go about one-third of the way, and stop buying properties after about ten years, you will still end up with over $5 Million in real estate, and over $26,000 per month in income.

So, this is also one of the most flexible of the Ten Other Real Estate Investments.

Section 121 and Section 1031 are the two best Sections of the Internal Revenue Code, and you can use them to create whatever level of wealth you desire.

You just have to do it.

CHAPTER 7

MOBILE HOMES

OVERVIEW

If more people were able to keep an open mind, the field of Mobile Home investing would be a lot more crowded. As it is, a relatively small number of investors are making very large returns investing in Mobile Homes.

But first, a little background.

Mobile Homes are more correctly referred to as "manufactured housing."

They are manufactured in a factory and transported either to a dealer, or directly to a location referred to as a "mobile home lot."

The size of the Mobile Home is from 10 to 16 feet wide, and from 40 to 80 feet in length, and dependidng a lot on the year of manufacture. The most popular size is 14 by 70 feet.

The destination/location for the Mobile Home is called a "lot" and is designed specifically to accommodate the Mobile Home, usually with a concrete pad to rest on, and with connections for utilities such as water, gas, electric, and sewer.

The mobile home lot might be inside a Mobile Home Park, and be one of 20-50 such lots in the Park. The amount of the rent will depend on the quality of the Park and the market demand for the area, but will normally be $250 to $450 per month. The national average is $300.

Or the Mobile Home location might be a separate lot in an urban or rural area similar to a residential lot.

The mobile home lot is not likely to be inside the city limits since most cities have strict zoning regulations which prohibit Mobile Homes.

The Mobile Home is classified in most States as Personal Property instead of Real Estate like a site-built house, and we'll discuss why this is important.

The mobile home lot, of course, is considered Real Estate.

In some States, the owner of the Mobile Home can file paperwork with the State to "convert" the Mobile Home from Personal Property to Real Estate, by "attaching" it to the mobile home lot.

Now, you probably already knew all that, but it's necessary to establish our starting point for discussion of the Mobile Home as a Real Estate Investment.

BUSINESS ENTITY

Read about business entities in Chapter 1 – Hard Money Lending. The same information applies here.

UNIQUE CHARACTER

Mobile Home investing is similar to some other forms of investing, such as Single Family Residences (SFR), Duplexes and Fourplexes, and Apartment Buildings, because it is providing a place for a person to live.

But Mobile Home investing is different, even unique, in four ways:

1.) Price.

2.) Land.

3.) Portability.

4.) Appreciation/Depreciation.

All four make Mobile Home investing different from other investing.

PRICE

The median price for a site-built home, meaning a three-bedroom, two-bath, two-car garage, on a residential lot, is $225,000, according to recent sales nationwide.

The median price for a new Mobile Home is $50,000. This does not include, of course, the lot on which the Mobile Home will be located.

If we deduct $25,000 from the price of the site-built home for the value of the lot, we can then compare the two straight-up, and we get a median value for the site-built home of $200,000.

Of course, almost all of the sales reported for site-built homes concerned homes that were no longer new, so the $200,000 would represent the median price of a used site-built home.

The median price of a used Mobile Home, in good condition, of recent design and appearance, is about $20,000.

That Mobile Home costs one-tenth (1/10) of what a site-built home costs, and that's a ratio of ten to one.

The price is what makes Mobile Home investing so attractive to investors.

A $100,000 site-built home being used as rental real estate might rent for $1,000 per month.

Ten Mobile Homes at a cost of $10,000 each might rent for $700 per month if they are sitting on their own lot. If they are located in a Mobile Home Park where the lot rent might average $350 per month, then they might rent for $300 per month.

Either way, the gross income from a Mobile Home rental is either three times as much or seven times as much as the gross income from a rent house.

LAND

The Mobile Home must have real estate on which to sit. That's obvious.

If you invest in Mobile Homes, that unit will usually already be located on either a lot in a Mobile Home Park, or on property that is owned by the owner of the Mobile Home.

Some investors only buy and sell Mobile Homes that are already located in Mobile Home Parks so that they do not have to be involved with the buying of the land that is under the unit, which can be complicated and a much more expensive transaction.

Mobile Homes are usually titled as Personal Property, and it is much easier to buy and sell them, as well as lease or finance them.

Other investors will only buy Mobile Homes that are located on real estate which they can also buy, which is usually land located outside the city limits. The investors prefer this because the used Mobile Homes that have decreased in value to the under-$20,000 range will not be going back up in value. They will not appreciate. But the land on which they are located probably will continue to go up in value. And asset appreciation is a key element of real estate investing.

More on this later.

PORTABILITY

Even though they are movable, Mobile Homes tend to remain where they are for long periods of time, even though the ownership often changes.

It is reported that five years is the average time for a Mobile Home to remain either in a Mobile Home Park or on private property before it is moved.

Personally, based on my many years of observation, I believe it is a lot longer, probably ten years.

Mobile Homes can only be moved on the highways by companies that are licensed to do so, and that have the necessary equipment and personnel. These companies are also the ones who are able to detach the Mobile Home correctly from its present location, package it correctly for transportation, and then set it up properly in a new location.

The price for the service depends on the distance and other factors, but is currently in the range of $2,500 to $3,500 for a single-wide and about $7,000 to $9,000 for a double-wide.

So, while the Mobile Home is certainly portable, the circumstances and cost of the move will often dictate that it remains where it is.

In most cases, an investor can buy a Mobile Home already located in a Mobile Home Park for less than what it would cost to move one there.

APPRECIATION/DEPRECIATION

The Fair Market Value (FMV) of anything is usually determined by the equation of Supply and Demand.

In some cases, it can also be influenced by calculating the cost of replacing the item either by construction or manufacturing.

Mobile Homes tend to sell in the range of $40,000 to $70,000 when new, and after eight to ten years, have a market value around $20,000 and less, depending on the part of the country and the immediate surroundings.

A well-maintained ten year-old Mobile Home in a nice Mobile Home Park, or on the water or a golf course, can go even higher than $20,000, but would probably not be of interest to the average Mobile Home investor.

You'll see why in the next Section.

The Mobile Home investor will be dealing in Mobile Homes priced from about $3,000 up to $12,000 depending on whether the deal includes real estate, and how much it includes.

In these cases, the Mobile Home will not appreciate in FMV over time. It will only increase in FMV if there is a measurable amount of rehab or repair work done.

But if the Mobile Home is located on real estate instead of being on a rented lot, the real estate itself will appreciate in value, in all likelihood.

Sometimes when you find a Mobile Home located on rural land, you will also find three or more Mobile Homes on the same land, sharing a water well, or a paved driveway, and in some cases sharing an aerobic septic system.

Some investors prefer the additional return on their investment of having the investment appreciate, and they prefer the Mobile Home with land included.

INCOME, PROFIT, AND RETURN

The nature of Mobile Home investing dictates that there are usually three types of investors, or rather, there are investors who engage in three types of activities.

An investor might choose to do only one, do two, or do all three.

The activities can be described as:

1.) Flip.

2.) Keep.

3.) Finance.

FLIP

The idea of the Flip is very simple.

A Flip is when the Mobile Home investor buys, and then sells quickly, for cash.

Buy the Mobile Home as cheaply as possible (see Finance below).

Sell it for as much as you can get, in cash, as quickly as you can.

Spend as little as possible on it during the process.

Your Buyer will be someone who will repair the Mobile Home, or improve it in other ways, and sell it to a new owner, either for cash or by providing the financing, or will do a clean-up to make the Mobile Home more attractive, and then rent it for income.

You can Flip in one of two ways.

You can act like the Wholesaler that we discussed in Chapter 4 on Wholesaling, and just assign your Purchase Agreement to a new Buyer in return for a fee.

Or, you can enter into a new Purchase Agreement with the new Buyer and schedule the Closing to take place immediately after the first Closing in which you purchase the Mobile Home.

This is called a Simultaneous Closing, but is actually a Back-to-Back Closing.

KEEP

The Keep is when you buy the Mobile Home and keep it, usually for the purpose of renting it out and creating rental income.

If you intend to sell the Mobile Home, it will be done under the third scenario below, called Finance.

The purpose of a Keep is to create income, nothing else, because the Mobile Home that you will be purchasing will have depreciated to the level where the value has leveled out, and will not be going down more, or going up.

The Keep is all about the numbers.

The returns on an investment of this kind will average about 40%, and can go as high as 70%.

A $100,000 site-built home in a subdivision might rent for $1,000 per month and provide you $300 per month cash flow, after deducting expenses, and adding back depreciation. That's on a $30,000 cash outlay, for your down payment.

For that amount you could buy six Mobile Homes.

A $5,000 Mobile Home in a Mobile Home Park will rent for an amount that is about $600 minus whatever the lot rent is. If the lot rent is $350 per month, which is about the average, the tenant can usually afford to pay $250 per month rent. For the investor, about $200 of that will represent net income, and since there is almost no depreciation, the $200 also represents the amount of cash flow.

I have not found the source of the information, but I have read a couple of reliable reports that $200 is the national average in net income for Mobile Home rentals.

But from a cash flow perspective, the Mobile Home can often provide a 25-month pay-back of the entire original cash investment of $30,000 for six Mobile Homes.

For Return On Investment (ROI), the $200 per month times 12 months times 6 Mobile Homes is $14,400 annually for the first two years, for a total of $28,800.

This is an Annual ROI of 48%.

After the 25th month, the entire investment has been returned, and the Annual ROI after that is infinite, because it is $14,400 divided by zero.

I will explain in Finance, below, how the investor can sell a Mobile Home for twice what he paid for it even though Mobile Homes do not appreciate in value.

FINANCE

The Finance activity involves buying a Mobile Home in good condition, cleaning it up, selling it to a new Owner, and financing the transaction.

The concept of Finance is all about cash – how much you have, how much the Buyer has, and how much you end up with.

First, you have to buy the Mobile Home.

And cash is king.

You determine the price you are willing to pay for the Mobile Home by determining what similar Mobile Homes are selling for in your area, and then take half of that average sales price amount. Then you deduct $500 for clean-up costs, and that is what you are willing to pay.

It is not negotiable. You either buy it for that, or you move on to the next one.

You can take this hard position because you are an investor who is willing to pay cash, and you are able to close quickly.

You are not taking advantage of anyone. This is just your business model.

There are people who, because of a transfer, job loss, death in the family, or pending divorce, to name just a few reasons, want and need to sell for cash right now.

They need you, and you need them, and your business model will work, for a number of reasons.

1.) Banks do not like to make loans on Mobile Home that are older than three years.

2.) Other potential Buyers who might compete with you for the purchase of this Mobile Home usually will not have the cash to deal.

3.) Most investors avoid Mobile Homes because they feel there is a social stigma attached to them.

You want to buy at between $2,000 and $3,000, spend about $500 on clean-up, and sell for $5,000 to $7,000.

And you want to do it quickly.

The economic reality of the market is that the potential Buyer will be concerned with only two things – how much down and how much a month. And someone who just doesn't have $1,000 to put down might still be someone who will make every payment once he is in.

It's a decision for you to make at the time.

But we will assume that we can get $1,000 down payment.

Assume that we bought for $3,000 and spent $500 on clean-up, and now we are selling for $7,000.

The next question is about the Note.

What is the term, what is the interest rate, and what are the payments?

We start at the end and work backwards, because the amount of the payments will determine whether or not we have a Buyer.

But sometimes he is also adamant about the interest rate, even though he does not understand how it will impact his payments. Few of us do.

So we pick an interest rate that sounds low to the Buyer, say 9.3%.

Now we figure his payments; not from the Note, but from what he can afford.

If you think he can afford a total of $600 a month for his housing expense, deduct the lot rent from this amount and you have his payment. If the lot rent is $350, he can afford to pay $250 a month on the Note.

Plug $6,000 as the Principal, 9.3% as the Interest, and $250 as the monthly payment into your Amortization Calculator, and you get a term of 26 months at $250 and a final month at $162.50.

You will be receiving total payments of $6,662.50.

Add the $1,000 down payment, and you will be receiving $7,662.50.

You bought the Mobile Home for $3,000 and spent $500 for clean-up, so your total invested is $3,500 plus holding cost and transaction costs, which can't be known at this point, so we will assume $500.

For a $4,000 investment, you will be making $7,662.50.

This is a profit of $3,662.50 which is an ROI of 91.6%.

Discount the Future Payments to Present Value, and it is still 81.5% ROI.

MANAGING YOUR BUSINESS

How you manage your business will depend on what your business model is, whether you decide to do one, two, or all three of the above activities.

Either way, you will be concerned about four things.

1.) License.

2.) Time required.

3.) Skills required.

4.) Money required.

LICENSE

Some States might require that you have some type of License if you are selling more than a certain number of Mobile Homes within a certain time period, usually one year.

You should follow the law.

But I have to tell you that from my experience, the requirement is very lightly enforced, if at all. I still recommend getting your License if the law requires it, but be prepared to compete against investors who do not follow the law, and might therefore have an advantage over you in some regards.

An advantage of being licensed anyway is that it might allow you to avoid paying the Sales Tax and the Title and Tag fee when you purchase a Mobile Home that you intend to sell, by just transferring these to the new owner, who would be paying again anyway.

You might also be in a State where the holder of a Dealer License is not even required to transfer title to himself when the Mobile Home is purchased, but can hold the title and transfer it from the previous Owner directly to the new Buyer.

That advantage alone is worth having the License.

Having a License also give the appearance of respectability in a business that could use it.

TIME REQUIRED

The question of how much time is required is answered by how much you want to do, and by how much time you have.

This is not a 40-hour-per-week activity unless you want it to be.

With each of the three activities, you can do very well with two deals a month.

And even as a Beginner, you should be able to do two deals in a total of about 15 hours.

SKILLS REQUIRED

For Mobile Home investing, the skills are exactly what you would expect them to be from what I have described to you thus far.

You absolutely must be able to work with people in a non-judgmental, friendly, and positive manner. Everything is flexible, everything is negotiable, and everything has a mid-point at which you can accomplish what you want, and the other party can receive what they need.

You must understand math, especially business math, which you can learn.

It would be even better if you could learn Bookkeeping. And eventually you will, if you stay in the business.

Mobile Home transactions involve a large measure of law and regulations, but it is the level of legal knowledge that you can learn, usually just by doing it a few times. There are some very good resources to assist you with this.

And, fortunately, there are some very good books that will tell you all you need to know to invest in Mobile Home, at any activity level.

You can choose one for yourself, but I would suggest that you ignore all of the others and buy a copy of "Deals On Wheels" by Lonnie Scruggs.

It is not new, and he has written another one since, but I believe the original is better.

You will like Lonnie, and I hope you buy his book.

MONEY REQUIRED

The requirement for money, like time, depends on your level of activity.

I will assume that you are a cautious Beginner, meaning that you will do as many deals as you can find that meet your criteria and comfort level.

If you intend to target the $7,000 Mobile Home, and do the Finance activity, which I would recommend in this economy at this point, you will need access to about $20,000.

You will buy for $3,500 and need $500 for clean-up and holding costs.

So, each deal will require $4,000 cash.

You should start with $20,000 and nothing less.

If you start with only $4,000 or $8,000 you might find a deal or two and then have no money until your Notes start bringing in payments.

With $20,000 and a cautious approach, by the time you use that up with five deals, payments on your Notes will have brought you another $8,000 and should be producing about $1,000 a month, so that all of your future deals will be funded by the Note payments.

Lonnie has a very good explanation of this in his book.

CONCLUSION

For the time and money required, Mobile Home investing is by far the most profitable type of Real Estate Investing you could be doing.

There is much more to it than I am able to describe here, and I recommend that you buy "Deals On Wheels" by Lonnie Scruggs for the details. And after you have read that one, buy his second one, "Making Money With Mobile Homes."

I also recommend that you read the other Chapters in this book to learn about all of the different ways that you can invest in the world of real estate.

CHAPTER 8

BILLBOARDS

OVERVIEW

Looking at all of the possible real estate investment assets, this one is the smallest, cheapest, and requires the least attention.

And yet it still rents for hundreds of dollars a month.

And very few people know about it as an investment.

Most of the value of a Billboard is not in the asset itself, but in the permit that allows the Billboard to be located where it is.

To invest in Billboards, you must focus on location first, and then look at the business and financial aspects of the deal.

REGULATION

Billboards are the only Real Estate Investment that are completely regulated by the government.

The regulator might be the United States government, State (capitalized for clarity) government, county government, city government, or all four.

By law, Billboards are only allowed in certain locations or zones, and the governing body of that location or zone has total control.

Now, this might seem like a deterrent to investing in Billboards, but just the opposite is true.

This restriction is actually a guarantee for you that once you secure a permit for one of these locations, everyone else is prohibited from competing with you there.

You have the exclusive right to have a Billboard in a specific authorized location, and everyone is excluded from placing a Billboard within a certain number of feet from your Billboard.

If a company wants to advertise to customers passing that particular location, then they must advertise on your Billboard.

No other type of real estate investing offers you what amounts to governmental protection against competition.

This gives your investment a built-in value factor that does not depend on income or occupancy or construction quality.

And the right is transferable, so you can sell it.

BUSINESS ENTITY

Read about business entities in Chapter 1 – Hard Money Lending. The same information applies here.

BUSINESS PLAN

As you know, with almost all real estate investments, the prevailing wisdom is that the three most important considerations "are location, location, and location."

It's a slight exaggeration, but still pretty accurate.

With Billboards, location is not just a consideration, it is critical to the entire concept.

You cannot put a Billboard where it is not allowed by law, so location becomes your starting point in the entire process.

The first thing that you must do is learn your local laws regarding Billboards, as well as your State laws.

And you proceed from there.

LOCATIONS

The location that you want, obviously, is a location beside a road or highway, because your Billboard message will be directed toward the drivers of the vehicles traveling on those roads.

The best location will be the location with the most vehicles passing in front of it.

But you won't have to count cars.

These traffic count numbers actually exist and are updated regularly. They are measured in number of vehicles passing a particular point per 24-hour period.

The entity doing the counting is the State, and it maintains a list, and produces a map of your area with the traffic count numbers displayed at various points on the major and secondary routes.

Each State has a different procedure for you to obtain the map, but you should start with the State Department of Transportation (DOT) website, and follow the process.

If you are totally stymied, visit the City Manager of your city.

TARGETING

After you find the highest traffic count locations, divide them into two categories, based on whether they are located in the city, or outside the city in the county.

This will determine who, in addition to the State, has jurisdiction over the Billboard.

Be aware that in some States, cities are permitted to have what is called "extra-territorial jurisdiction."

This means that the city might also control Billboards located within a mile or two of the city limits even though the Billboard is physically located in the county, which will also have jurisdiction.

Now you must review the city ordinances and the county ordinances as they relate to Billboards.

You are looking for a high traffic count location coupled with an ordinance that will permit construction of a Billboard.

Start with all of the locations for which you can obtain a traffic count, instead of just the ones that you think look best.

It takes very little additional time to do all of them, and you really don't know enough at this point to make the decision concerning which ones to focus on.

SORTING

Now it is time to get on your pony and ride.

But first, check and see if your State's transportation department maintains a public list of all licensed Billboards within its borders. If so, that list will have at least some valuable information for you, and it might have a lot.

And while you're at it, download an Application and any supporting documents so that you will know exactly what is in store for you if you go through the application process.

Now, get in your vehicle, take your map, list, and your notes, along with a camera, and drive to each of the locations on the traffic count map.

Look at the Billboards that are already at the location.

This is your starting point.

Now look at the ordinances and determine if there are any additional Billboards authorized in addition to the ones that are there, and if so, how far away, sizes allowed, etc.

Don't be discouraged if there are no more permits available for the location. That just means that you will be considering buying one or more of the Billboards that you see instead of building a new one.

Make extensive notes on all of the locations, and make two lists, one for potential purchases, and one for potential builds.

Also make note of whether the Billboards are lighted, as this is a significant factor.

And be aware that if you decide to compete in this location, you will be coming back at another time, putting on your boots, and walking to the Billboards and inspecting them, taking notes and photos, and checking out the electrical service, as well as the vehicular access from the nearest public road.

All of the Billboards owners will have obtained a legal right of access to the Billboard from the nearest road, so try to find that access if you can.

INCOME POTENTIAL

At this point, you need to just go to the end of the investment and work backwards.

Before you can make decisions about buying or building a Billboard, you need to determine what income you will be receiving.

All of the rest of your decisions will be based on the expected income to be produced by the Billboard.

You need to know the rental rates for the Billboards.

The easiest way to find this is to call the phone number on the Billboard and ask for a rate card.

You might also find a website identified on the Billboard, usually the owner/operator or the advertising agency handling the account.

Go to each website and get as much information as you can.

Go through this process for every one of the Billboards that you are looking at, careful not to repeat a contact.

This will give you a good idea of the "rate card" in effect for your area. Be careful to note the different rates for different sizes and types of Billboards. This is your learning process for making decisions in this industry.

If you live in an area that is large enough to have a regional advertising agency, go to their website and find the rates for the Billboards that they are handling, and any other information that seems relevant.

CONSTRUCTION

A basic Billboard built with telephone poles can be done for about $5,000 and there are plenty of companies to do the work.

And there might be some locations where this is the proper method of construction.

But the best investment in terms of holding the value and always being in demand will be a Billboard constructed with metal.

And with modern manufacturing techniques and milling standards, the components will be cut and prepared at the factory and trucked to the site to be assembled.

You'll have a much better asset.

To maintain the market demand for your Billboard, you want to stick to the four basic sizes.

1.) 6' X 12' (called an 8 sheet poster),

2.) 12' X 24' (a 30 sheet poster),

3.) 14' X 48', and

4.) 10'6" X 36'.

You can expect to spend about $1,000 for the process of obtaining a permit or license. It could be more if you are required to have an engineering study or report to accompany the Application.

To find out the cost of construction for various types of Billboards in your area, you just contact the construction companies that do this type of work and talk to them.

MANAGEMENT

Managing a Billboard investment is nothing like managing a rent house or managing an apartment building. By comparison, with Billboards, there is really nothing going on.

Once the advertiser puts up the ad, you just receive the checks for the 6-month or 12-month period of the lease.

Unless you are managing the Billboard advertising yourself and targeting local advertisers, you will place your Billboards with an Advertising Agency and pay the 15% commission.

This is usually the better use of your time, and will open up your potential advertiser list to regional and national advertisers, as well as relieve you of the sales, marketing, bookkeeping, and accounting duties.

It will also increase your chances of renting the Billboard because the clients of the large Advertising Agencies usually buy a number of locations at one time in a focused area or along a stretch of road, and the Agency can bundle your Billboards with others to provide this package.

Your expenses will be few.

1.) If you are using an Advertising Agency to rent your Billboard space, there will usually be a 15% commission charged.

2.) If you are lighting your Billboard, there will be a monthly utility bill.

3.) You should carry an insurance policy on your Billboard to cover casualty losses, but not a liability insurance policy because it will only attract frivolous lawsuits.

4.) There might be a license fee levied by the municipality, or they might just be happy collecting the property taxes.

5.) You want to be the one who takes down the expired sign, usually vinyl, and installs the new sign. You can pass the cost on to the advertiser, but you want to control the access to the property and the quality of the work. The company that prints the sign will usually offer this service as well, but you will need to monitor the quality of the work.

6.) You will have regular inspections of the Billboard and surrounding area, and do maintenance whenever necessary. You can do this yourself or hire a company to do regular landscaping and inspection, notifying you when it appears that repairs might be needed.

ACQUISITION

Whether you buy or build, an important element of the deal will be the land.

You won't need a lot, but make sure that it is large enough to contain the sign itself plus enough additional space all around the sign for a fairly large truck to drive.

You will need this for the construction, if you are doing that, and for maintenance if you are buying an existing Billboard. The truck will have a crane mounted on the bed and will have outriggers to anchor the entire truck and crane.

In addition, make sure that you also acquire an access easement between the Billboard location and a public street or road.

If the land will be leased instead of owned, make sure that the Lease term is for at least ten years, with at least one, and hopefully two or three renewal options on your part.

As for your business model, although you will probably build some Billboards when you know more about the business, and when you find a great opportunity, in the beginning you will probably be buying your Billboards.

One single Billboard will not do much for you starting out. In the beginning you want to start with at least three, and as many as twelve.

To do this you need to find a company or an individual with a number of Billboards, where you can buy some of them or all of them.

Every owner of multiple Billboards has a few that he "would just as soon get rid of."

Look at your ownership list if you got one, and look at the notes that you took during your inspection tour, noting which Billboards seem to be neglected or needing attention, or maybe even abandoned.

Make a list of the Billboards that you want to target for acquisition.

The prices for the Billboards will vary for every place in the country.

You can pay between $1,000 and $30,000 for a Billboard, but will probably be operating in the area of $5,000 to $15,000 for a quality Billboard in a good location.

These should rent for about $375 to $400 per month, with about $75 to $100 a month in expenses.

TAXATION

You will have two types of taxation, the taxation of the income produced by the Billboards, and the property tax that will be assessed yearly on the Billboard itself, either as real property or personal property, and maybe both, depending on local laws.

You might also encounter a license fee that is being imposed by a municipality, that is nothing more than a disguised tax, but is legal anyway.

The taxation of the income from the operation of the Billboard investment will depend on the ownership of the Billboard.

If you own it in your own name, then the income will be taxed at your personal income tax rate, after a Qualified Business Income (QBI) tax-free income deduction of 20%.

If you own the Billboard in a Pass-Through Entity (PTE) it will benefit from a 20% tax-free deduction of income, and the remaining 80% will pass through to you and be taxed at your personal income tax rate.

Pass-Through Entities are LLCs, S Corps, and Partnerships.

CONCLUSION

The monster, tall two-panel, double-sided, digital Billboards on the beach drive in Miami or Tampa with a 68,000 traffic count can certainly cost $350,000.

But these are not what we are talking about.

The Billboards that you are likely to be investing in are also not in Baltimore or Cleveland, or any major city.

Your Billboards will be outside of a medium-sized, or smaller, city and have a 12,000 to 20,000 traffic count, on a major State highway or bypass.

The Billboard will rent for about $375 per four weeks (this is the rental term, not a month; so you receive 13 annual payments), and you will have to pay about $125 of that for commission and expenses.

So, you will clear 13 x 250 = $3,250 per year.

Not a lot of money, but about what you would be getting on a $50,000 rent house, and about half of that would be spent on repairs and remodeling when the tenant moved out.

But with this Billboard, you can probably buy it for about $8,500.

That's an annual ROI of 38%.

Most Billboard investors will not consider a deal unless it returns at least 20%.

For $100,000 you can own about a dozen Billboards, with a monthly income of about $3,000.

It's not passive income, but almost.

If you want a healthy return on your investment, and don't want to deal with all of the hassles of rental property, investing in Billboards could just be what you are looking for.

CHAPTER 9

STORAGE UNITS

OVERVIEW

The Storage Unit industry is unique among the many platforms for Real Estate Investing.

There are about 40,000 facilities in the U.S.

You have probably seen the very large operations in your area, and if so, you probably think that they represent the entire industry.

But they do not.

These large operations are usually owned by Real Estate Investment Trusts (REITs) or other very large syndicators.

They represent only about 10% of the total market.

The other 90% are owned by medium and small investors.

About 65% of all owners will own a single facility, and about 25% will own two, three, or four. The remaining 10% will be the large national companies with many facilities.

The industry has not consolidated, and it will not. There are too many business models, and there will always be a niche for the medium and small operator, because there are so many customers.

Currently, about 10% of the U.S. households are renting a Storage Unit, and the average number of units rented by each customer is 1.3.

The average unit size is 120 square feet.

This customer base is made up of two groups.

About 80% are individuals, and about 20% are businesses.

In the first category, in addition to the typical homeowner, your individual customers will be students, military personnel, apartment dwellers, divorced persons, new people arriving in town, and people moving to other towns.

For a relatively low price, you are providing the customer with space to store items which they value very highly.

And your business is almost immune to market fluctuations. The market demand for Storage Units will not be affected by the economy, at least in a negative way. The demand is steady in both good and bad times. In fact, business usually increases in times of economic disruption because individuals and businesses are making changes and need temporary space for storage.

Your strongest customer base will come from a five-mile radius of the facility.

I'll have more on that later. It is critical.

There are many different types of facilities:

1.) Basic Dry Storage Only.

2.) Climate-Control.

3.) Basic RV and Boat storage.

4.) Mixed.

Storage Units are the least complicated of all residential or commercial real estate investment property.

BUSINESS ENTITY

Read about business entities in Chapter 1 – Hard Money Lending. The same information applies here.

STRATEGIES

Unlike apartment buildings, or strip shopping centers, there is a lot of flexibility in operating a Storage Unit facility.

You can almost make it anything you want it to be, as long as the market will support it.

Your basic facility will have the usual number of units, called Dry Storage Units.

They are just metal boxes on a concrete slab, usually with a garage door type of entrance.

The facility might also have climate-control units, which will maintain the temperature below 90 degrees in the Summer and above 40 degrees in the Winter, and maintain the humidity below 65% at all times.

These units require a little more investment, and therefore are rented for 30-40% more.

In addition to the metal units, you will have space surrounding the buildings, which you can rent for other purposes.

The most common is for Boat and RV storage.

There are five types of Boat and RV storage services.

1.) Open Space – sizes vary from 10x20 to 12x50. They are laid out and numbered.

2.) Covered Space – open space with a cover.

3.) Covered Canopy with Walls – covered space with two side walls, and sometimes also a back wall.

4.) Enclosed Space – usually the largest because they are intended to be used for the most expensive Boats and RVs, which are the largest. They might include climate-control and electrical service.

5.) Condo – these are separate units, usually 14 feet wide, and they cater just to RV and Boat owners who want a special unit where they can be comfortable while caring for their toys.

In addition to the storage units and the space for Boats and RVs, the facility might provide any number of other services for the production of income.

1.) Truck rental.

2.) Trailer rental.

3.) Boxes, tape, labels, packing material, etc.

4.) FedEx drop-off location.

5.) Mailboxes.

6.) Safety Deposit Boxes.

7.) Car wash.

8.) Billboards.

9.) Cell phone tower.

Income and cash flow are usually the major reasons for an investor buying a Storage Unit facility and holding it long-term.

But, the potential is huge for buying or building a facility, managing it up to 80% occupancy, providing a year of financial records, and then selling. Under ideal circumstances you could double your money.

If this is your Business Model, you could be doing one about every 18 months and doubling your money each time.

Although there has been a lot of growth in the industry, there is still room for more investors coming in.

As I said, the industry has not consolidated, and will not. Facilities are owned by investors, and there are many different types of investors with different goals.

CHOOSING A FACILITY

The first, and most important, thing for you to decide is what type of facility you would like to own, and focus your search on that particular type.

If you are open to any type, or almost any type, then your search will be easier.

But you must choose a market area in order to be able to analyze the facility as an investment.

Make sure that the market numbers look good.

Look at the number of households within a five mile radius of the area you have chosen.

Look at the total demand for Storage Units within that market, and then look at the portion of that demand that is already being supplied by the existing facilities that serve the market.

You want to find a market area that is under-served.

Within that market area, you want to find a facility that has two main characteristics.

The first characteristic is that the facility is not being managed as efficiently as you could do it.

The second characteristic is that the facility has enough available land that you can use to alter and expand the operation. It is far easier to build additional units on an existing facility than it is to build an entire facility at once.

While you are managing the facility up to maximum profitability, you can be adding rows of units for the untapped demand that you have identified.

Your best chance is to buy a facility with 300-500 units because the big investors are not interested in anything smaller than 750 units, or at least 500 units with enough room to expand to 750-1,000 units.

But with 300-500 units, you will still be attractive to the large number of middlemen who are buying this size facility and expanding with additional units, including climate-control, and Boat and RV parking, and selling the project to a Real Estate Investment Trust (REIT), or even syndicating the project themselves.

Or you might even be considering doing something like this yourself.

The average unit size should be 105-125 square feet.

About 60% of the units should be 10x10 or smaller.

An average mix is:

20% 5x10

10% 10x20

25% 10x15

40% 10x20

5%   10x25

These are just numbers that give you an idea of what is happening in the industry, but not necessarily where you are.

But for a typical 500-unit facility, the mix might be:

5x5 (20)

5x10 (75)

10x10 (125)

10x15 (70)

10x20 (100)

10x25 (40)

14x20 (10)

10x30 (40)

12x25 (5)

12x30 (5)

10x40 (5)

14x30 (5)

Your income per square foot on the smaller units will be about twice what is will be on the larger units.

I won't go into the financing of your purchase, because the subject is too extensive to cover here, but I would like to point out one thing that might help you.

The Small Business Administration (SBA) now guarantees loans for Storage Units.

And also, you should use an Analyzer software program for your first deal. There are many available.

BUY OR BUILD

Building a real estate investment is almost always better than buying an existing facility.

Your costs will be about 30-40% less.

Construction, after all, is the process of taking building materials stacked on the ground, combining it with labor, and producing an asset capable of producing cash.

You create economic value. The results, the whole, is always worth more than the sum of its parts.

So, the best investment in the Storage Unit industry would be one that you build.

But if you choose this route, you should contract with one of the major national builders to do the work.

A local builder will be less competent and will not have the buying power to get the lowest prices on material, or have access to workers who are good at this type of construction.

Metal building construction is about $9 per square foot for a metal building with a standing seam roof.

The metal building contractor will supply you with the plan and instructions for the concrete contractor, who will be familiar with the process because he has handled other similar jobs.

Based on an 80% occupancy rate, you should have your loan paid off in about six years, including the land purchase, materials, and construction.

If you already own the land, that time is reduced to three years.

You can develop a facility for about 1/3 to 1/2 what it would cost to build a comparable Multi-family or commercial facility.

You could be your own General Contractor, manage the project, and hire the sub-contractors.

But you should be aware, if you have not built a large project before, at least a Fourplex, or a Mobile Home Park, or something on a similar scale, you probably should stay away from this route.

Either way, real estate construction is not something that you can learn by reading about it, or even taking courses. About 80% of the knowledge and ability is gained through experience.

And although they might claim to be telling you the "secrets," real pros keep the secrets to themselves. That's how they make a living. It's their security, and they are not giving it away.

So, in all likelihood, you will be buying an existing facility.

In that case, you need to first find the market, and then find the facility.

To figure out how to do both, see the following Section on Managing Your Business, specifically the information on customers, income, and expenses.

MANAGING YOUR BUSINESS

One of the primary attractions of Storage Units for many investors is the fact that although you are still dealing with the public, with all of the problems that usually presents, with Storage Units, these people are not living on your property.

You are not responsible for their safety, comfort, and welfare, except while they are visiting. You are providing no personal care or services, but the checks are coming in every month.

CUSTOMERS

I don't like the idea of placing a "lifetime value" on a customer.

I think it is a very mercenary approach, and disrespectful to the customer.

But it does demonstrate how very important the customer is to the Storage Unit business.

And it has been determined in the storage industry that the lifetime value of a customer is $3,500.

This is because most customers originally plan to rent a unit for maybe three or four months, and end up keeping it for 18 to 24 months. It's just too much trouble to close it, even if they later have somewhere to put their stuff, which they usually don't.

Statistics show that almost all of the customers for Storage Units come from within a 5-mile radius of the location of the facility.

So, after making sure that the facility is located on a road with at least 20,000 vehicles passing by each 24 hours, you must define your market area.

The local government and/or the State will have collected data on the number of vehicles passing the location within specified time periods.

You will get your customers from three main sources.

45% saw the facility while they were driving by.

35% found the facility on the internet.

20% were referred by other customers or businesses.

And the reason that you must define your market area is to determine how many potential customers you will have, based on the number of households within the 5-mile radius of your facility location, your market area.

About 10% of U.S. households currently rent a storage unit, and the average number of units rented by each customer is 1.3 units.

The average size of the rented unit is 120 square feet.

You can find a lot of data online about the number of households in specific areas, and this might be good enough for you to get an idea of the income potential of the project that you are considering.

But when you get to the serious stage, you should hire a company that will produce a very detailed report for you.

INCOME

In the 1960's when Storage Units were first maturing as an industry, the rent rate was about fifteen cents per square foot per month.

By 1985, this had gone up to sixty cents.

By 1998, it had gone up to $1.00.

Today, the range is $1.50 to $4.00 per square foot per month.

You can find out what the rental rates are for your area just by calling and asking. Call different facilities and ask about different units – dry, climate-control, RV and Boat storage, etc.

This will allow you to start with the potential income of a Storage Unit facility, and work backwards.

You should try for 80-85% occupancy. That seems to be the norm. If it is more than that, your rents are too low for the market.

The climate-control units will be interior units, and should rent for about 30-40% more than the dry units.

Storage Units are rented month-to-month, so you can raise rents anytime that you want.

You should raise rents at least every six months, and sooner if your occupancy rate goes above 85%.

The amount of the rent increase should be twice the increase in your operating expenses for the same period. That way, you are maintaining your profit margin, at the same time that you are increasing your income.

The amount of annual income is more important than just for determining the amount of money you will have to live on.

The appraised value of the facility, the amount you would be able to sell it for, is based on the annual income.

So you should be constantly working to raise that number.

EXPENSES

Your actual expenses will depend on the type of facility and the location.

But there are typical expenses that you can expect, such as:

1.) Advertising.

2.) Personnel – a facility as large as 50,000 square feet will require a full-time manager.

3.) Repairs and Maintenance.

4.) Insurance.

5.) Utilities.

6.) Property taxes.

7.) Other – office supplies, credit card fees,

Although depreciation is not an expense, it is an allowable deduction from income. With Storage Units, depreciation must be claimed over a 39 year period, not 27.5 years as it is with residential rental property.

The best thing about your operating costs is that they are very low, but the second-best thing is that they are completely predictable.

That means that you can operate on a budget and do projections that are likely to be very accurate, unlike most businesses, where the unexpected is always happening.

Except for a natural disaster, which will be covered by insurance, there will be no large expenditures.

And if your operating costs are predictable, so is your net income, a situation that you won't find with other real estate investments.

Everything will depend on your occupancy rate.

You will have regular increases in your costs of labor and supplies over time, probably 3-5% per year.

But you can easily cover these increases by just raising the rent. Increasing rent for storage units is easier than for any other type of real estate investment.

No one will go to all of the trouble of moving to another facility just because of a $5.00 per month increase.

But if you multiply that $5.00 times 500 units, you've just added $30,000 to your annual gross income.

So your annual increases should be enough to cover your annual increase in costs, plus an equal amount to increase your net income.

Remember, increasing your net income will increase the value of your facility.

EMPLOYEES

If you own a 500-unit facility, with the mix that we described earlier, you have 80,000 square feet of storage space.

Anything above 40,000 requires a full-time on-site manager.

With an investment this size, especially in the beginning, you will probably want to be the Manger.

And to take care of the extra hours when you are not able to be there, and the days which you will not work, you will probably also need an Assistant Manager.

This is the person you would train to take over when you step away from the business, or who stays with the business when you sell it.

You can afford to hire someone who is highly qualified on the business level, and who is an outstanding person, because your facility will be generating strong income.

With an 80% occupancy rate on 80,000 square feet, you will have 64,000 square feet rented each month, and if your average rental rate is only $3.00 per square foot, you will be bringing in $192,000.

So you are not competing with McDonald's and Pizza Inn.

Some Managers like to handle the front desk. I do. It is the most important job in the business.

Your competitors have the same units for rent that you have.

You compete with them by treating customers like you appreciate them and like you are the answer to all of their needs. For every happy customer that leaves your office, three will return because of word-of-mouth.

But if you can find a desk clerk who is very good, you might want to just remain in the office and manage the business.

In addition to someone to run the office, you will need three or four maintenance people. They will do cleanup, and regular inspection of units.

TAXATION

For information on taxation, please read the Taxation section of Chapter 1 Hard Money Lending.

CONCLUSION

As I said in Overview, the Storage Unit industry is unique among the many platforms for Real Estate Investing.

Whether it is right for you really depends on your personality, where you are in your investing life, and where you want to go.

There is no way that I could give you a blueprint, nor that you could follow one to success.

I have tried to give you enough information and insight to decide if you are interested in pursuing the idea.

At this point, you should continue to gather information, and there are two sources that I would recommend.

Be sure to read material available from the Self Storage Association (SSA). It is the newest and most relevant.

The other association, Inside Self Storage (ISS), also has training material. Their website is SelfStorage. org.

Good luck.

CHAPTER 10

RAW LAND

OVERVIEW

Land investing is different from all of the other forms of real estate investing.

There is no building or structure involved, so land is easier to evaluate, purchase, and manage.

The major attraction of buying land for investment is that it involves so little effort. Unlike rental properties, land doesn't constantly require your time and money.

There are almost no recurring expenses, as the land just sits there. It requires no rehab, no repairs, and it doesn't wear out or depreciate.

Once you buy it, you're not "on the clock" to turn it into a cash-flowing asset, like you are with rental income property, which requires "income."

Land can be much more flexible for meeting whatever your financial requirements are in regard to creating or handling your wealth.

For example, you can use land as a store of wealth, instead of holding your wealth in paper money or precious metals.

Most of the land that I bought doubled in value every ten years, even if I did nothing to it.

But you also have the option of making limited improvements to the land, and turn it into an asset with a stream of income that could help cover your cost of financing. You can clear and fence it, and then lease the land for farming or grazing.

Or, you can completely change the character of the land, creating another type of land in the process, such as putting a road through 100 acres, cutting out 20 5-acre tracts, and selling each tract for three times your per-acre cost of acquisition of the 100 acres.

One of the principals of land sales is that the smaller the usable tract, the higher the per-acre price.

Land can become many different investments, depending on what your needs are, and based on your available resources of time and money.

Let's break it down and look at it.

INCOME

You won't find a real estate asset with more flexibility than land.

When you buy a rent house, for instance, you have a single asset, and that's all you will be able to make it.

When you buy 100 acres of land, you can divide it into as many assets as you want. Each asset can be a different size and shape, used for a different purpose, leased or sold for cash or for a note, or just left alone to grow timber.

Some land investing books promote the business model of buying land that is vastly underpriced, and then selling it at its Fair Market Value and making a profit.

Good luck with that.

Does it happen?

Of course. I've done it.

But it is not a business plan. It's a hope. Vastly underpriced land is hard to find, and the amount of time that you spend looking for it will not be justified by the eventual profit you make.

If you expect to receive income from land, it will usually be:

1.) Hunting leases, or

2.) Lease for pasture for animals, or

3.) Lease for farming, or

4.) Sale after increasing the quality or character of the land, or

5.) Sale of smaller tracts after dividing, or

6.) Harvesting timber at 15-year or 25-year intervals.

Some of these options will not be available in your area, and others will not be practical, and others might be more than you wish to be involved in.

The most common method of producing income from raw land is a combination of increasing the quality of the land and then dividing it into smaller tracts for sale.

IMPROVE AND LEASE

But if your business model is to do basic improvements to the property and then lease it for income, you should consider the person who raises cattle, or wants to get into the cattle business.

They usually start with a few cows and a bull. You know how that works. And then they sell the male calves and keep the females, building up their herd.

They need land. They probably can't make a profit just starting out if they have to buy the land. But they will lease your land and pay you according to how much grass it provides for a certain number of months for a certain number of head of cattle. The market rate for the area will tell you what this price is.

The Lessee might even agree to fence the land as part of the deal.

DIVIDE AND SELL

If your business plan is to buy a large tract, clean it up, divide it into smaller tracts, and sell these, you need to start with the eventual sale, and work backwards.

Study the market to determine the prices of land of various sizes. This is where your advantage lies. Find out the per-acre price of a small tract, and compare that to the per-acre price of a large tract. The difference will be where you generate your profit.

What you will probably find is that 100 acres, on a county road, mostly level, part woods and part clear, with electricity and water service available, will sell for about $200,000.

But $200,000 still sounds like a lot. Yet, it is only $2,000 per acre.

You can sell one acre all day for only $2,000.

But you wouldn't make any money.

And you actually can't sell all of them for $2,000 each.

The lots with road frontage will sell for much more, and the ones without road frontage, which means without access, will sell for a lot less, if at all.

EXPENSES

The expenses of investing in land will be tied directly to whatever you intend to do with the land.

If you just intend to hold it long-term, maybe thinning the timber a couple of times and then cutting all of it, then there will be almost no expenses involved.

You will need to pay a Forester to assist you in managing the timber crop, but this will be one of the best investments you will make, and his fee will come out of the sales proceeds. The timber business is a jungle, and you will definitely need a professional representing you.

If you intend to sell the land, either as a total tract, or after dividing it, you will probably have to clean it up.

That involves labor and equipment.

You can purchase the smaller equipment, and you can hire some of the unskilled labor. But you will also be looking at hiring large equipment like bulldozers and mulchers, along with the operators.

It can be expensive, but having a fence, culvert and driveway, gate, and a cleared road and building site can double your asking price, because your property will look better than anyone else's, and it will be "turnkey," ready to use and enjoy.

Virtually every expense that you have with investing in raw land will result in the market value of the land being immediately increased by more than the cost.

So, when thinking about investing in land, think about what it will cost to get the property into your name, and what it will cost to make the property exactly what a large number of people are looking to buy.

Once you make a sale, you will have the added expense of paying for a Survey, Title Insurance Policy, and document preparation and closing costs.

But these will come out of the Gross Sales Proceeds and you will not have to pay them in advance in order to get to the closing table.

CASH FLOW

Land will usually not create a cash flow for you.

Hunting leases will pay some small amount, but not nearly enough to justify the amount of liability you will be assuming.

Pasture and farming leases are the best possibility, and if you want to own land for the long-term and have some periodic income, this is probably the best area for you to look into.

As for timber, although it does not really amount to cash flow, if you planted pine or hardwoods on land with an average quality soil and harvested after 30 years, following one or two thinnings, and then pro-rated the income back over the period of your ownership, it would probably amount to $25-40 per acre per year.

That probably would not put it at the top of your list of investments, but, on the other hand, you still own the land after 30 years, and it has probably gone up in value about five times. So, it could be a consideration.

If you sell the divided parcels and do Seller Financing as I explain below, with one of the three methods where you do not have to pay off the underlying debt, you will create a cash flow that can be calculated as the difference between the payments you are receiving and the payments that you are still making on your own note.

Many investors do exactly this, with the goal of accumulating about 30 or 40 Promissory Notes with monthly payments coming in.

APPRECIATION

Land values will be determined by the supply and demand.

You can rely on the old adage "They are not making any more land" if that approach gives you confidence to invest.

But, in a way, they are "making more land," if you are talking about land that is available for purchase and that people want to buy.

In fact, it is one of the things that you will be doing yourself after you buy your land, as I explained above in the section on Income.

But land values will also be determined by another element of supply and demand, and that element is "money."

If you are holding your savings in cash, you should consider owning land as an alternative.

Paper money has no intrinsic value. It's paper. The value lies in the willingness of another person to accept it in exchange for goods and services.

For example, your $200,000 in savings will buy 100 acres of quality land at $2,000 per acre.

It is much more likely that more money will be printed than it is that more land will be developed and marketed.

So, if the money supply increases and you have more dollars chasing the same amount of land, that 100 acres could go up to $3,000 per acre in a year or two. I've seen it happen when the stock market gets shaky.

So, your 100 acres just increased in value 50%.

If you were holding your $200,000 in savings, there is no way that it would increase in value 50%.

In fact, when that 100 acres increased in value to $3,000 per acre, your $200,000 in cash will now only buy 66.67 acres, so your cash actually went down in value in relation to the land.

The government will always be printing more money, as the economy expands, or when it falters and requires stimulation, or even a bail-out. It's what they do.

And each time, your paper money becomes less valuable through loss of buying power.

But that 100 acres of quality land cannot easily be duplicated.

Every day there are more dollars chasing the same amount of land.

The law of supply and demand will cause the value of the land to steadily increase.

LEVERAGE

The concept of leverage applies differently to Land Investing than it does to rental income investing.

The value of land is based more on the market supply and demand, whereas the value of rental real estate is based on its ability to produce income, and what it would cost to replace the asset.

Therefore, land value is less likely to be affected by the factors that affect the value of an income property.

As a result, land value is likely to be more steady, and as a result, the lenders are inclined to loan a higher percentage of the purchase price.

In a healthy economy, the standard down payment required to purchase raw land is about 10%.

So, you are able to use a higher degree of leverage in land investing than you are able to use in rental income investing.

TAX ADVANTAGE

The tax advantages for normal real estate investing come from the Depreciation Allowance that turns part of your income into tax-free income, and the crazy IRS rule that dictates that the rental income is passive income not subject to the 15.3% Self Employment Tax.

There are others, but those are the main ones.

But with land, there is no depreciation, and there will probably not be rental income, so those tax advantages do not exist.

And since you will probably be dividing a large tract into multiple smaller parcels for sale, you are operating as a Dealer, as the IRS views you.

You are selling products and the parcels are your inventory.

So the income will be ordinary income, and will be taxed at your ordinary marginal income tax rate.

There are ways that you can operate as an LLC and elect S Corp status, paying yourself a salary which you deduct as an expense of the operation, and then drop the profit through to yourself as the shareholder, and this last amount would not be taxable as Self Employment Income.

But that is a longer discussion for another time.

BUSINESS ENTITY

Read about business entities in Chapter 1 – Hard Money Lending. The same information applies here.

BUYING

When you are buying land, it is a good idea to lie. But only about your reason for buying. Be truthful otherwise.

If the owner even has a hint that you intend to make a profit selling the land, he will keep it, confident that the person you intend to sell it to will come along next month and offer him more than you are offering.

You should say that you are buying it to leave to your kids because you worry that they will never have anything on their own. He will identify with that.

But spare him from making the mistake of holding onto the land for the wrong reason.

PROPERTY CHARACTERISTICS

When you buy land, you are not able to rely on all of the knowledge that you have acquired by dealing with other real estate, knowledge that would assist you in choosing a rental property, for instance, because you've lived in those properties and you know everything about them that you need to know.

But land is different, especially if you've never bought or sold land before. You can't rely on your knowledge or your instincts.

Here are the factors that you must consider when buying land.

1.) Location.

2.) Divisibility.

3.) Access to a public road.

4.) Available water.

5.) Available utilities (electricity, gas, sewer, etc.).

6.) Available public services (fire protection, police, mail delivery).

7.) Terrain/Topography.

8.) Drainage.

9.) Soil quality.

10.) Real estate taxes.

11.) Availability of quality tenants.

12.) Woods/pasture ratio.

13.) County statutes.

Depending on your business model, each of these will carry different weight. You must determine the order of priority, depending on your business model and your target customer.

THE CONTRACT

Spend a lot on time on the Contract.

The Contract is your entire deal, reduced to writing.

Whatever you plan to do, you must make sure that the Contract is written in such a way as to allow you to do that.

Look at Chapter 4 Wholesaling > Buying for a good explanation of how to handle the Contract. It has everything that you need to know.

THE OFFER

This is the key to your success.

Even more than the Purchase Price, or the location, or the property taxes, or the topography, the Offer that you make will determine whether your project eventually turns out successful.

The Offer will include the Purchase Price, of course, but it also includes other things that might turn out to be much more important.

You should haggle on the Purchase Price, because the price that you begin with is often just the Asking Price. The Seller doesn't expect to get that. He uses that number so that he can be talked down to the price he is actually willing to take for the land.

But don't haggle too much.

Take your time, go back and forth, and when you get to where you think the Seller's real price is, then you start to deal with the other items that are even more important.

Here are some of the things that you want.

1.) Owner Financing. If you have cash, use it. Once the land is in your name, you can then go to the Bank and get an Investment Loan with the land as collateral. But the Bank will be much harder to deal with than the Owner regarding a Partial Release and the Due On Sale clause, which we will discuss later. The best business model for land investing is for you to only use about $30,000 of your own money and try to buy land in the $100,000 to $200,000 range. Standard Down Payments are 10%, so you use part of your funds for that, and the rest for improvements and marketing. But it is critical that you focus all of your effort on getting Owner Financing. You can even offer to pay a higher interest rate. People love to brag about having a note paying them 9.7%. But for you, since the amortization period will be 25 or 30 years, you will not be paying a lot more with a 9.7% note than you would with a 4.5% note. You might even offer to sign a Note for 11.7% in return for a $10,000 reduction in price. That gives you more money to work with up front, and you will not be making these payment for more than four or five years anyway. Personally, I would pay full price for land every day if I could also get Owner Financing, along with the items that I have listed below. You might also put a balloon payment in the Note after five years, telling the Seller that he gets all of his money in five years, a very attractive prospect for him. You can afford to do this because if you are dividing and selling the tract, you will have finished all of your marketing efforts within that period of time, and if you have not, it will be easy to get financing for the remainder, and just hold it for appreciation.

2.) Partial Release Clause. You want the Seller to agree to release smaller tracts if you pay him a pro-rata price. For example, if the remaining balance owed on the 100 acres is $180,000 and you want to cut out and sell a 10-acre tract, you pay the Seller $18,000 and he signs a Partial Release of Lien on the property that describes that 10 acres that is released from the Deed of Trust lien that is on file in the county Real Estate Records. In selling this 10 acres, you would probably be receiving $30-35,000 gross, so you are probably making $9-15,000 profit on the transaction, after expenses.

3.) Due On Sale Waiver. You want to be able to sell some of these smaller tracts on an Installment Note payable to you, without first having to pay the Seller for a Partial Release. So, you want the Seller to agree that as long as he still has a First Lien on the total acreage still subject to the lien, he will allow you to do this type of "Wraparound Mortgage."

4.) Survey. Require the Seller to provide you with a Survey. That is the normal way that land sales are done. However, this is a great area for you to negotiate, and both you and the Seller benefit. If the Survey will cost $5,000 that means that the Seller will have that deducted from his proceeds at Closing. Tell the Seller that you will pay for the survey if he will reduce the price another $4,000 and he comes out $1,000 ahead. He will probably do this. You pay the $5,000 for the Survey, but you pay $4,000 less for the land, so you are getting a Survey for $1,000. It will be well worth it. The additional advantage you receive is that this allows you to deal with the Surveyor directly yourself. You can negotiate with him to provide the paid-for Survey for the entire tract, and then provide a second Survey that is identical except that he marks the lines dividing the tract into whatever configuration you think will give you the most flexibility for marketing the property. You could do a 20-acre tract and ten 8-acre tracts, or whatever. For the Surveyor, once he collects all of his data for the original Survey, the extra work will be done at his computer, and he will probably be willing to do the extra tracts for about $500 each, including a legal description for each. I've done this for even less, so if you cannot negotiate a deal, shop around for another Surveyor.

5.) Down Payment Deferral. Instead of offering a $20,000 Down Payment and a $180,000 Note at 9.7% for a $200,000 property, you offer to sign a Note for $200,000 and put $20,000 into Escrow at Closing to be used to do improvements on the property, like cleaning the ditches, installing culverts and access drives, fencing the entire tract, and clearing appropriate areas for homesites. As each improvement is completed and paid for, a receipt is presented to the Title Company or Closing Attorney holding the money in Escrow, and that amount of funds are released back to you. You can do it in about $5,000 increments and eventually get back all of the $20,000 which you have put into improvements on the property, something you were going to have to do anyway. You can agree that any escrowed funds not used after 24 months go to the Seller as a reduction of principal on the Note. This has two benefits. You are able to use all of your funds for improvements and marketing, and the Seller will see the property that is securing his $200,000 Note go up in value by at least $20,000 and probably more because of the improvements, making him more secure in case he has to foreclose. And he still gets his entire $200,000.

There might be more items that you want to negotiate, depending on which business model you decide to use, but the Offer is where you set these terms, and make sure that they are included in the Contract.

EARNEST MONEY

I know I've covered this in the other Chapters, but since each Chapter covers a separate subject, and this might be the first Chapter that you read, it's part of the explanation.

Earnest Money is what the Buyer "puts up" to guarantee that he will go through with the Contract, and not just say, "No, I've changed my mind," walk away, and leave the Seller with nothing but a lot of wasted time.

If the Buyer does not go through with the Contract, the Earnest Money is given to the Seller as compensation for wasted time, expenses incurred, and lost opportunity.

The Earnest Money is deposited with the Title Company, and is held in Escrow by the Title Company under the terms of the Contract, and is disbursed by the Title Company as dictated by the Contract when one of the parties to the Contract defaults on the Contract, as "default" is defined in the Contract.

There are two points that you need to pay very close attention to now.

The first point is that most Buyers think that they have covered their backsides by putting contingencies in the Contract that will guarantee that they can back out of the Contract and get their Earnest Money.

Don't count on it.

When the Title Company accepts the funds, the Title Company becomes what the law defines as a Fiduciary.

A Fiduciary is an entity that is holding money that belongs to someone else and is responsible for its safekeeping and correct disbursement.

As a Fiduciary, the Title Company can be sued for not disbursing the money to the right party. Because of this liability, the Title Company is entitled to require each party with a potential claim on the funds to sign an "Instructions To Disburse" document directing the Title Company exactly how the funds are to be disbursed.

What all this means is that if either party contests the disbursement requested by one of the parties, the Title Company will inform both parties that the Title Company does not have the authority to decide who is right, and that it will only disburse the funds with a Court Order.

In the fifteen years that I ran my Title Insurance Company, I never disbursed Earnest Money over the objection of one of the parties to the transaction.

Does this mean that, as a Buyer, you should not deposit any Earnest Money, or that you should only deposit a minimal amount? No, quite the opposite.

And that brings us to the second point.

The second point is that as a Buyer you should not be concerned with avoiding liability for not going through with the Contract. If you did your homework, and you negotiated a good Contract, you should very much want to go through with the Contract.

If it is a Contract that you think you might have to walk away from, you probably shouldn't be doing it.

Also, if the unforeseen should happen, and you are unable to continue, the Seller deserves to be compensated for his time, expenses, and lost opportunity.

MANAGING YOUR BUSINESS

Since you are not dealing with tenants and toilets, the management of your Land Investing will depend on which business model you choose.

For buying and holding there will be almost no management.

For leasing for pasture, you just find the tenant, sign the lease, and collect the monthly rent.

For dividing into smaller parcels and selling, you will be running a business. You create your products, then you market your products, and when you sell the products you might be engaging with the Buyer over a period of time if you are doing some type of Seller Financing.

TIME REQUIRED

As you can see, there is no way to predict the amount of time that will be required for Land Investing.

It will depend on what type of investing business model you choose, and it will depend on your own activities.

For instance, if you are a real estate sales agent, you could do this at the same time and require very little additional activity.

But if you are working as a Pharmacist, and doing this in your spare time, it could require all of that time, and might even prove impossible to do if you are trying to divide and sell smaller parcels.

It would also depend on whether you decide to do the sales and marketing yourself or just sign a Listing Agreement with a realty company.

I think I have given you enough information in this Chapter to estimate what your personal time requirement would be.

SKILLS REQUIRED

You need basic business skills to do this.

And you need a willingness, and probably an eagerness, to learn about land ownership and land use. Your knowledge of the product will be your primary asset.

In addition, you will need people skills, if you are dividing and selling parcels. Understanding the Buyer's needs and wants, and meeting them, will lead to your success.

BOOKKEEPING

Since there is not a stream of income, nor monthly expenses, to keep track of, you will not really be concerned with Bookkeeping.

Just keep all of your receipts, and document all of your transactions.

ACCOUNTING

If you are buying and holding for investment, just document your purchase, keep receipts for your monthly and annual expenses, and complete the tax forms necessary.

If you are leasing the property, you will have income and expenses, and you will have annual taxable income. Keep all receipts and complete the annual tax form.

If you are dividing and selling parcels, you will need to find a Bookkeeper who can explain the requirements to you, and who can help you with reporting your income and expenses on your tax return, maybe even setting up a system for you to follow.

LIABILITY

There are two types of liability that you should be concerned about.

The first is personal liability where a legal cause of action might result in a lawsuit against you, which might result in a Judgment against you, which will probably result in a lien being placed on all of your assets, causing a sale of assets to provide funds to pay off the Judgment.

The second type is financial liability. This goes to who is responsible for paying the debt on the property, and who is responsible if the property is sold and does not provide enough funds to pay off the debt.

With Land Investing, both should be a concern for you.

To deal with personal liability, you should make sure that you do not own the land. The land should be owned by an LLC which you own. That way, if there is a claim arising from an accident or other event on the land, the claim will be asserted against the LLC and not against you.

To deal with financial liability, you do the same thing. The holder of the debt might require you to personally guarantee the debt, and if that is the only way that you can hold the property in your LLC, then you will have to guarantee it.

TAXATION

As I explained earlier, the income from the leasing of the land will be ordinary business income, and will be taxable at your ordinary income marginal tax rate.

The income derived from dividing the land and selling parcels will be ordinary business income, and will be taxable to the entity which owns the land. If it is a Pass-Through Entity (PTE) such as an LLC, Partnership, or S Corp, then the income will be taxed to you personally.

SELLING

You might only be interested in buying land and holding it to take advantage of the anticipated increase in value, or you might only be interested in the land as a method of storing your wealth instead of holding it in paper money.

But most of the time, the purpose of buying is to be able to sell.

So, you need to understand who is buying, besides you, of course.

The buyers of land can usually be divided into three categories.

1.) Individual buyer.

2.) Single investment buyer.

3.) Institutional buyer.

Since your business model will probably be to purchase a large tract and divide it into smaller tracts and sell those, you are in the second category, and your buyer is most likely to be the first on the list, the individual buyer.

Look at Property Characteristics above to see what you should be looking at in selecting your property.

And look closely at the possible buyer.

If the buyer is someone who can work from home, his home can be 30 acres in the country with a view of the mountains, or 15 acres bordering on a river.

Have a clear idea of your possible buyers in mind when you are looking for property to buy, and plan accordingly.

If you want to target the largest group of buyers, and you probably do, you will have to provide the option of Seller Financing.

The largest group of buyers will be people who do not have the cash or the savings to buy outright. They will have two questions.

1.) How much down?

2.) How much a month?

These two concerns are more important than even the price, so if you offer good financing, you should be able to sell at top prices.

A cash buyer, of course, can reasonably expect you to transfer the land to him, free and clear, which means that you would have to use part of the sales proceeds to pay off the underlying debt and get a Partial Release of Lien.

But this group of buyers who require Seller Financing will accept the situation where they are not receiving clear title immediately.

You have three options.

1.) Lease With a Purchase Option. This is a lease of the land in which the Lessee pays a monthly lease amount with the understanding that at a designated date in the future he will have an Option to purchase the land at a specific price. Sometimes the Lease will stipulate that 15% of each payment will be credited to the eventual purchase price. These arrangements are totally flexible and can be tailored any way you like.

2.) Contract For Deed. This is a Contract in which you do not transfer title to the property, but receive payments each month toward the purchase price, and when a certain total amount has been received, you deed the property free and clear.

3.) Wraparound Mortgage. This is where you sell the tract to the Buyer, but "subject to" the financing lien that is already in place, and you add a second lien that you can foreclose on if the Buyer does not make the payments as outlined in the Note and Deed of Trust. If he does make all of the payments, then you must pay off the underlying debt and deed the property to him free and clear.

This is why it is important for you to start with the selling of the property and work backwards to the buying of the property. That's the only way you will be able to get everything to work.

CONCLUSION

Land investing is really so many different investments that it is not possible to cover everything in this one Chapter.

The subject really requires a complete book.

I recommend that you go to Amazon.com and look at the books by Pat Porter. He is the best. He has the knowledge, and he has the ability to communicate the information to you.

I hope that I have been able to provide you with enough information for you to grasp what this type of investing is all about, and for you to determine if you want to pursue it further.

This is one of the types of Real Estate Investing that I will be engaging in over the next five to ten years, and when I do, I plan to write a book devoted solely to land investments.

Meantime, I hope that you have seen the potential in it that I have seen, and that you will choose to pursue it.

Good Luck!

CHAPTER 11

CHARGING ORDERS

OVERVIEW

Whatever method of investing you choose, you will need to do it through a business entity in order to shield yourself against personal liability and shield your assets from levy and foreclosure.

To understand this better, I refer you to my book "How To Choose Your Best Business Entity For Real Estate Investing: LLC, S Corp, C Corp, Partnership, or DBA."

Most of you will choose to invest with an LLC, and there is a great deal of confusion concerning exactly why you are doing it.

So, I've included a Chapter on the primary benefit aspect of the LLC, called a Charging Order.

WHAT IT IS

A Charging Order (CO) is an Order issued by a Court and signed by a Judge, directed to an individual or legal entity that is holding funds, or controls the distribution of funds, for a second individual.

The Charging Order directs the individual or entity holding the funds to transfer the funds to a third party instead of transferring them to the individual who owns them.

This comes about when there has been a lawsuit filed against the owner of the funds, and the lawsuit has resulted in a Judgment being granted against the owner of the funds, and a lien being placed on his assets.

The holder of the Judgment lien is called the Judgment Creditor, and the party against whom the Judgment is entered is called the Judgment Debtor.

The Judgment filing creates a Lien on all of the non-exempt assets of the Judgment Debtor.

But if the asset involved is an ownership interest in a Limited Liability Company (LLC) or a Limited Partnership (LP), then the asset cannot be taken (in most States).

That's where the Charging Order comes in.

The unique feature of the Charging Order is that it does not grant the Judgment Creditor the right to receive the asset, but only the right to receive payments or distributions that the Judgment Debtor would receive that represents the income produced by the asset.

So, the Charging Order is a court-ordered lien on the distributions, but not on the asset.

Charging Order protection is not available for the entity itself if the entity is sued and has a Judgment granted against it.

HOW IT WORKS

For Example, you and your brother are contractors, and together you set up an LLC to run your business.

But your brother gets into financial trouble with a personal debt, is sued, and has a Judgment entered against him for $100,000.

It is not a Judgment against the LLC, but your brother owns half of the interest in the LLC as one of his assets. And his assets are subject to being taken to satisfy the Judgment.

However, under the Charging Order protection, the interest in the LLC cannot be taken, only the distribution represented by the interest.

So, if the LLC makes $120,000 in the tax year, you and your brother will each receive a Schedule K-1 (1065) for $60,000 of income.

(You did not file Form 8832 electing the way in which you wanted to be treated for tax purposes, so you were give the default category of Partnership by the IRS).

But since your brother is not entitled to receive his $60,000 of income because of the Charging Order, his Schedule K-1 is sent to the holder of the Judgment Lien under the terms of the Charging Order.

WHY IT IS VALUABLE

However, the Charging Order does not actually require that the distribution of the income be made to the holder of the Judgment Lien, the Judgment Creditor.

The Charging Order requires that "when and if" the distribution is made, it must be made to the Judgment Creditor instead of your brother, the Judgment Debtor.

And the Charging Order does not give the Judgment Creditor any voting rights or any other rights regarding the LLC.

Also, a copy of the Schedule K-1 will be sent to the IRS identifying the Judgment Creditor as the Taxpayer entitled to receive the $60,000 of income.

The IRS will expect the Judgment Creditor to report the income on his personal tax return and pay the taxes on the $60,000 of income, even if he did not actually receive the income.

If the Member Managers of the LLC, which are you and your brother, decide not to distribute your brother's portion of the income, the Judgment Creditor will end up paying thousands of dollars in taxes on income that he may never receive.

Then you can go through it again next year.

Eventually, he will release the lien on the LLC interest, or, more likely, his Attorney will not file for the Charging Order in the first place.

This is why Charging Order protection is valuable.

HOW IT COULD FAIL

The laws concerning the Limited Liability Company (LLC), the Limited Partnership (LP), and the laws concerning Charging Orders are different for each State.

In some states, the Charging Order is seen as a protection device for those owners of an interest in an LLC and LP who have not had a Judgment Lien filed against them, but one of the other interest owners in the LLC or LP has had a Judgment Lien filed.

In other states, the Charging Order is seen as a reasonable and responsible business rule, and should be afforded to all owners of LLCs and LPs.

Wyoming, Delaware, Texas, and Nevada are probably the best, but first let's discuss the worst.

There are some states that even deny Charging Order protection to Single Member LLCs (SMLLCs). I discuss those below.

There are 15 States which will allow the holder of the Judgment Lien to petition the Court for permission to foreclose on the LLC and LP interest, claiming that the Charging Order is not a reasonable solution.

In addition to allowing judicial foreclosure of the LLC and LP interest, some States also provide for the appointment of a Receiver. This is a disaster for both parties, as the Receiver may just try to keep the matter going for as long as possible and collect the fees.

But you can protect yourself against these situations.

If you operate in one of the States with weak Charging Order protection, you can create the LLC in that State and have it own the real estate.

But you can have the LLC created in that State owned by another LLC that you create in a State with strong Charging Order protections, like Texas, Wyoming, Delaware, or Nevada.

This way, you don't own the LLC that owns the real estate.

You own the LLC that owns the LLC that owns the real estate.

Then, when there is a Judgment Lien against you, the LLC interest that you own is an LLC formed in a State with strong Charging Order protection, and your interest in that LLC cannot be taken.

You can only be subjected to a Charging Order, and you can just leave the income in the LLC that your LLC owns. Even though it is in a State with weak Charging Order protection, it is safe because it is owned by your LLC, not by you, and so it is not affected by either the Judgment or the Charging Order.

The Charging Order can only be against the interest that the Judgment Debtor owns in the LLC created in the State with strong protection, and that State does not allow foreclosure or the appointment of a Receiver.

And both LLCs can just retain the distributions, but send the Schedule K-1 to the holder of the Judgment Lien so that he can pay the taxes.

The Nevada LLC owns the LLC that owns the real estate. You own the Nevada LLC. The Nevada law on Charging Orders protects your Capital Interest if you are sued.

SINGLE MEMBER AND MULTI MEMBER

A Limited Partnership (LP) will always have more than a single member. It will have a General Partner and one or more Limited Partners.

But an LLC can be either a Single Member LLC, called a SMLLC, or a Multi Member LLC, called a MMLLC.

And in addition to the States with weak Charging Order protections, there is another problem with some other States.

Some States do not provide the same Charging Order protection to SMLLCs that they offer to MMLLCs.

Charging Order protection is denied completely to SMLLCs in:

1.) California,

2.) Colorado,

3.) Georgia,

4.) Florida,

5.) Kansas, and

6.) New York.

On the other hand, States with statutes that clearly say that the Charging Order is the only remedy available to the holder of the Judgment Lien are:

1.) Nevada,

2.) Wyoming,

3.) Delaware,

4.) South Dakota, and

5.) Alaska.

The statutes and the court cases of the remaining States fall somewhere in between these two extremes.

Some books claim that Nevada and Wyoming have allowed bypassing the Charging Order protection for SMLLCs, but this is not true.

The two cases cited in the books by authors hawking their services and claiming to be knowledgeable about this, were not based on the LLCs having single members instead of multiple members.

The two cases involved a Bankruptcy in one case, and a case of piercing the corporate veil due to blatant undercapitalization and irresponsible manipulative management in the other.

The verdicts would have been the same if the entities had been MMLLCs.

So you might want to decline the huckster's invitation to pay his "affiliated agency" a thousand dollars to show you how to gift 5% of your LLC to your child through the Uniform Gift To Minors Act, or set up a Revocable Trust, not even a legal entity, so that you will not be a SMLLC.

CONCLUSION

The Limited Liability Company (LLC) is getting old enough to have some solid case law to explain it and back it up. And the true social and political attitudes of the various States are becoming pretty well established.

It looks like there will be 15 or 20 States that will not be friendly to the LLC form of business.

But it looks like there will be an equal number where the LLC will exist as it was originally intended, as a reasonable limit of liability for businessmen willing to incur the expenses and risk the uncertainty of operating a business.

Right now, there are about five strong LLC environments.

1.) Nevada,

2.) Wyoming,

3.) Delaware,

4.) South Dakota, and

5.) Alaska.

In the past couple of years, at least three other States have amended their LLC statutes to almost copy the Delaware statutes.

And two of those State are pushing to establish the types of Business Courts that Delaware has, where business cases are heard by Judges who actually know what is going on, instead of Judges that hear divorces, criminal, juvenile, and everything else, and just don't understand a lot about the real world of business.

The friendly business environments in Delaware and Nevada are providing huge amounts of revenue for those State governments, and some of the other States are paying close attention.

Nevada, South Dakota, Alaska, and Wyoming also have the additional advantage of having no State income tax.

If you live in one of the weak States, you just have to deal with the situation, and decide how much risk you are willing to tolerate.

You might just want to use a separate LLC for each of your rental properties, and keep the loans as high as you can, so that there is as little equity as possible.

Or you might want to go ahead and operate with a Delaware or Nevada LLC and have it own the other LLC which are holding the real estate.

But you need to understand the situation, and make your decision.

CHAPTER 12

CONCLUSION

OVERVIEW

This was a very difficult book for me to write.

I was writing for about ten different groups of people.

So my message had to be consistent, but also had to be crafted for each individual.

The person with $20,000 to invest in Mobile Homes is not the same person with $300,000 who will be a Hard Money Lender.

And I have not had enough space in each Chapter to show you how to do the entire business model, although the ones on Hard Money Lending and Raw Land come pretty close, and I am thinking about doing entire books on those subjects.

What I wanted to do was show you the strategies and lifestyles involved with each type of real estate investment, and give you an idea of what your life would look like if choose to go that route, so that you could make the decision about spending more time to investigate.

I hope that I have provided you with some useful information.

If I have, I would very much appreciate it if you would go to Amazon and leave a review.

And if not, please contact me at:

Michael@MichaelLantrip.com, or my website:

MichaelLantrip.com, with your question or comment.

Thank you for being a reader.

10 OTHER REAL ESTATE INVESTMENTS

MICHAEL LANTRIP

Made in United States
Orlando, FL
11 May 2024

46739848R00136